Angel of Grief
William Wetmore Story
1894

DEATH BY EGO

What We Can Learn From Entrepreneurs Who Kill Their Companies With Hubris

by

David M. Carlson, Ph.D.

Frontispiece: Angel of Grief or the Weeping Angel is an 1894 sculpture by William Wetmore Story for the grave of his wife Emelyn Story at the Protestant Cemetery in Rome. Its full title bestowed by the creator was The Angel of Grief Weeping Over the Dismantled Altar of Life. This was Story's last major work prior to his death, a year after his wife. The statue's creation was documented in an 1896 issue of Cosmopolitan Magazine: according to this account, his wife's death so devastated Story that he lost interest in sculpture, but was inspired to create the monument by his children, who recommended it as a means of memorializing the woman. Unlike the typical angelic grave art, "this dramatic life-size winged figure speaks more of the pain of those left behind" by appearing "collapsed, weeping and draped over the tomb". https://en.wikipedia.org/wiki/Angel_of_Grief

For permissions contact:
DMC@Fuuse.com
www.DeathbyEgo.net
Cover by Author

ISBN: 978-0-98253-851-7
Published by
ProtoMet Media
www.protometmedia.com

Table of Contents

FOREWORD

"If you have an important point to make, don't try to be subtle or clever. Use a pile driver. Hit the point once. Then come back and hit it again. Then hit it a third time – a tremendous whack."

- Winston Churchill

The Book's Objectives and What's the Point?

The objectives of this book are straightforward:

- Alert potential investors to common characteristics entrepreneurs share so that investors may make better informed decisions and insist on strong governance.
- Provide true stories about entrepreneurs that failed their companies in order to provide material to entrepreneurial-study programs.
- Remind entrepreneurs about tendencies that may jeopardize their success and the success of their companies.

Background

In the last 25 years, at least 12,000,000 new businesses were created by entrepreneurs in the United States alone. It is estimated that 51% survive the first 5 years. The rest not only fail but take substantial amounts of capital with them. I've witnessed several of these failures firsthand. My hope is to provide some insight into underlying causes of what went wrong.

What is hubris?

First, a simple definition of "hubris:"

> **A "human character trait that causes an individual to believe and act as if his or her beliefs or positions are totally, absolutely and uniquely correct for a given situation or on-going activities."**
>
> **Or**
>
> **"An ancient Greek word meaning pride or arrogance, used particularly to mean the kind of excessive pride or conceit that often brings about someone's downfall."**
>
> **- Dictionary of Unfamiliar Words by Diagram Group**

A Greek playwright is believed to have said, "Every tragedy begins with hubris." This lesson is nowhere more apparent than in the situations described below.

Academic insight

In 2010, C.S. Carver and S.L. Johnson wrote and published a research paper, "*Authentic and hubristic pride: Differential relations to aspects of goal regulation, affect, and self-control*" in the Journal of Research in Personality (44, 698-703.) The conclusion was:

> "Overall, the differential pattern of correlations fits with a model in which authentic pride is tied to adaptive achievement and goal engagement, whereas hubristic pride is tied to extrinsic values of public recognition and social dominance."

Their conclusion that "hubristic pride" is tied to public recognition and social dominance is consistent with the anecdotal evidence below.

Inherent Conflict in the Entrepreneurial Process

Entrepreneurs create new ways of thinking about situations and opportunities which can only be successful and executed by abandoning some prior thinking and existing paradigms. So, successful entrepreneurs must have significant confidence in their new ideas. The danger is that this confidence can result in hubris if not balanced by a recognition that even great ideas may often be improved upon, especially with the coaching of competent colleagues and mentors. When there is no acknowledgement that the coaching of others may be helpful or even critical, they demonstrate the kind of hubris described in the stories below.

This comes to light at meetings of venture capitalists (VC) wherein entrepreneurs are invited to make presentations. After a question and answer period, venture groups often excuse the entrepreneurs and then the VCs discuss this question: Are these entrepreneurs coachable? The VCs will most often pass on the investment if they determine that the presenting group is deemed un-coachable. As coachability and hubris are antithetical, many venture firms understand the danger of investing in entrepreneurial hubris, so they choose to pass.

Lack of Hubris: A Definitive Example

Michael Faraday became Professor of Chemistry at the Royal Institute of Great Britain in 1833. His work was a monumental contribution to the world as described below.

> "Faraday is generally held to be one of the greatest of all experimental philosophers. Nearly every science is in his debt; and some sciences owe their existence mainly to his work. The liquefaction of gases, benzene, electro-magnetic induction, specific inductive capacity, lines of force, magnetic conduction or permeability, the dark discharge, anode, cathode, magneto-optics, electro-chemical equivalent; all these terms suggest fundamental researches which he made, and many of them were called into existence to describe his discoveries."
>
> - Sir William H. Bragg, Director -
> Laboratory of the Royal Institution (1932)

Faraday apprenticed as a bookbinder prior to his efforts as an experimental physicist exploring the relationship between magnetism and electricity. There is a story told that when his findings were published, he unbound the book and re-bound it with a blank page between every page of the original book. His logic was simple: he may have made a mistake or an oversight and there may be other ideas that compliment the ones that he'd outlined in the book and he wanted to make sure he kept track of them. This is the profound opposite of the characteristics described in detail in the following examples of entrepreneurial hubris.

Truthful but not Factual

All the events and observations described below are truthful in all material ways. However, many of the specific details have been changed for purposes of confidentiality. There is one exception: Dr. Henry C. Yuen. He is mentioned by name because his activities are well documented publicly and quite extraordinarily. In 2008, Dr. Yuen was declared as a "fugitive from justice" by the Los Angeles U.S. Attorney.

Structure of Scenarios

In the next few chapters, I've structured the examples in this way:

- Background to set the stage for the discussion
- My position at the time and how that allowed me to observe events
- The events themselves
- The results
- A perspective about the role that hubris played in those results

Corporate Hubris?

While this book focuses on individuals, there is one experience that provides an example of what might be called "corporate hubris" that I witnessed and will share. I attended my first meeting of officers at Kmart in 1985. In that meeting, Kmart's vice president of marketing declared that he just finished a new analysis of Walmart and concluded that Walmart was out of sites for new stores because they had exhausted rural county seats in the southeast. [The bad news was that I went short on Walmart stock that afternoon. The good news is I only lost $420.] In 1985 Walmart had sales of about $8 billion with about 880 stores and Kmart had sales of about $21 billion with more than 2,000 stores. In 2017, Walmart had sales of $485.9 billion with nearly 12,000 stores in 28 countries and Kmart continues to close stores.

In the 10 years I served as a senior executive at Kmart, I was never in a meeting that confronted the issue of how Kmart could, should or would change its strategies to fight the increasing Walmart dominance of the U.S. general merchandise discount market. Is it possible that Kmart was a pioneer in introducing the notion of 'corporate hubris' in 1985?

Something to Consider

Were these experiences a result of my long term and sustained naïveté or a reflection of the fact that entrepreneurial hubris and its devastating impact on companies is far more common than previously documented?

Commentary

A Psychoanalytic Perspective on Hubris

Every human being deals with his or her narcissism from birth but not every human being develops a narcissistic character structure. We are born with narcissistic impulses but also empathic impulses. They live in conflict but also in balance. Empathic impulses are impulses that feel inner pain when we see another suffer. As those impulses develop we build a capacity to put ourselves in the shoes of another and not only understand one's inner emotional situation, but also feel the urge to help alleviate the pain if we can. As a result, we develop an awareness as to how our actions affect others and we feel bad when they create pain in others. Our narcissistic and empathic impulses are like fluctuating breezes that pass through our emotional life. They are dynamic not static. It leaves most of us with the question: "If I am not for myself, who will be and if I am only for myself, who am I?"

However, for a person with a narcissistic character structure (often referred to as a Narcissist - the DSM-5 calls it a "Narcissistic Personality Disorder") it is qualitatively different. It's like the steel beams holding together a building. All that takes place inside that building is within the framework of that structure. A person that meets the DSM-5's definition of Narcissistic Personality Disorder (for these purposes call him or her "N") does not have the advantage of empathy. Empathy does not exist within that structure and by definition is void of empathy. In some cases and situations, of course it may be an advantage: one can operate without concern for others or worry about how one's narcissistic ambitions affect others. An N can fire people at will, not pay contractors and cheat stock holders out of money without any guilt or shame. An N does not have to deal with the human element at all, giving him greater freedom to advance his cause, free of humanistic burden. The N has a grandiose sense of self-importance, exaggerates achievements and talents, expects to be recognized as superior and is exploitive in relationships. Most Ns will lie, take advantage of others and do whatever they can get away with, to achieve their goals. This is where the absence of empathy helps. They don't have to feel bad about what gets trampled in the process. Psychology basically believes that once structured it can't be changed. A personality disorder can't be changed and is not accessible to Psychotherapy.

Because N has fantasies of unlimited success, power, brilliance, how special they are and how they should be treated as such, they feel they can get away with almost anything. Almost always the N will crash and burn at some point.

Certainly not all entrepreneurs are Ns, but being an N, unfortunately often helps. In this book, you have shown how Ns and "Hubris" are related. Your definition of hubris is certainly an N trait. Your examples are interesting in that they show how common this may be with entrepreneurs and how people get sucked into the charisma of an N. Your educating people about this potential disaster is not very different from my using psychotherapy to help a person in relationship with an N. Your showing how businesses are destroyed by Ns in the context of "Hubris" is something creative and new to me, but, unfortunately, makes perfect sense.

John VanDixhorn, Ph.D.

Psychoanalyst and Chairman,
Newport Psychoanalytic Institute (retired)

Chapter 1

Please Get Me a Bodyguard

"The measure of a man is what he does with power."

- Pittacus

Background

When the bank decided that Peter's company was in trouble with a negative net worth of more than $2.5 million and continuing operating losses, I was recruited by a board member to manage the company. I went in with both bank support and board support although I was unsure of support from the founder and his wife who were both board members.

The founder and previous CEO was a brilliant mechanical engineer who migrated to the United States from South Korea. He attended the University of Michigan where he got a degree in mechanical engineering. Over the years, he created very large automated food packaging machines under several patents. His design philosophy included the principle: a machine should never make noise because noise is a result of mechanical inefficiencies and produces wear. In fact, one could carry on normal conversations on the floor of the packaging operation where 16 massive machines were in full production because they were so beautifully engineered.

The company's primary business was to produce packages that cleverly contained single portions of sugar, salt and pepper. The company had a few large customers including an airline and a hospital supply wholesaler. The company's market share in health care and the airline industry was substantial. Unfortunately, it lacked cost accounting and incurred excessive labor overhead that resulted in selling product below cost. Additionally, the founder's wife (and a board member) hired friends from the community to tear open packages that were defective and reclaim the sugar. These efforts contributed to labor expenses higher than they needed to be.

Adding to the operating problems was a pressing liability of a $200,000 note owed to a Korean businessman in Los Angeles. The note was due within a few months. The lender was purportedly an associate of Tongsun Park who was one of the subjects of an extensive investigation into bribery of members of congress. Mr. Park had significant relationships with the Connell Rice and Sugar Company through banks in Washington and Bermuda and had bribed a member of congress for the U.S. government to arrange to use this company for shipments of goods to Egypt.

The company that Peter founded had other obligations including indebtedness associated with municipal bonds issued by the city and then used to purchase equipment and make improvements to the facility.

Position

I came into the company as CEO with four direct reports: Director of Operations, Finance Manager, Personnel Manager and a secretary. The first few weeks were spent learning as much about the underlying business and its economics as quickly as possible.

Events

During the first few weeks we created new packaging to sell sugar, salt and pepper packets through very attractive retail displays in grocery and convenience stores. Our plan was to sell them in packs of 10 and have them ready for Memorial Day picnics. The Company also had a sizeable printing operation so all the packaging for the individual servings of sugar, salt and pepper could be produced in-house. This printing asset allowed us to design and print new packaging within a week of developing the concept. The packaging machines could be set up for the new product within a few hours.

To renegotiate the terms of the $200,000 note I decided to go to Los Angeles and meet with the noteholder. When I talked to the VP of Operations about the trip to Los Angeles, he told me, "I guess you heard about the Monosodium Glutamate (MSG) contracts, right?" But I hadn't.

I then asked him to explain and when he realized that I did not know about this practice he disclosed that the company had been submitting false purchase orders for MSG to the company holding the note and then accepting and acknowledging falsified shipping and receiving documents for MSG. The final step was paying for the falsified shipments. I immediately suspected that these payments were in lieu of interest on the debt. In fact, this process would allow the lender to take costs against the payments thereby reducing or even eliminating his tax liability. Within a few hours I determined that no MSG was ever purchased or received. As of that moment the potential negotiations with the lender took a very different and ominous turn and I began to worry about my safety in Los Angeles. I began to feel that I should have a bodyguard with me on the trip.

I called a very good friend who had been a trial attorney for the IRS and had a thriving practice at a very large law firm in Detroit and asked if he could help me find a bodyguard for the Los Angeles trip. His counsel was simple, "If you feel you need a bodyguard, do not go." I took his advice and canceled my trip. After a few follow-up discussions, I retained him to do a full review of the MSG arrangement and to investigate any other transactions that might compromise the company. In the next few weeks he uncovered and documented seven areas in which the company had operated illegally. One of the more minor infractions was the founder's extensive use of company credit cards to pay for personal expenses including clothing and gym memberships for his wife, son and daughter.

When the investigations were complete and documented, I called a special meeting of the board at the corporate offices. I introduced the subject with the MSG story and then turned the meeting over to the attorney. After about two hours, the Chairman, a prominent Ann Arbor attorney who was totally loyal to the founder, decided to end the presentation we were making and adjourned the meeting. I strongly protested and asked that the meeting minutes show that the CEO had not had a chance to fully disclose the results of the investigation and give my recommendations. As a result, the meeting was reconvened the next day in the Chairman's law office conference room in Ann Arbor. After the board heard the full presentation, it rejected my two recommendations: 1) to fully disclose the findings to all related federal and local jurisdictions and, 2) immediately eliminate the board positions for the founder and his wife. I then resigned, as did the board member who had recruited me.

As a side note, one of the items that I was able to cover and confirm in the minutes of this meeting was that all employee withholding had been paid to the IRS through that date. This entry into the Corporate Minute Book became critical as the IRS took the actions described below.

The following Monday morning, the attorney and I took all the documentation to the IRS District office in Detroit, asked for the "Agent of the Day" and fully disclosed everything we had uncovered. The meeting took six-hours. After leaving copies and signing a document that attested to the fact that I had disclosed everything material that I knew, we left.

Results

The IRS, the bank and the city took several subsequent actions including indictment of the founder and seizure of his large estate and cars.

Several months after I resigned, the IRS determined that the company had not paid employee withholding since the board meeting described above and the board members were subsequently held liable for the withholding payments that had not been remitted by the company.

For my part, the company was obligated to provide a six-month severance because of an employment contract. However, until the severance was paid, regular salary payments were to be made. As a result I received 11 months of salary for seven weeks of work. I was happy with the pay but hated the whole experience.

The Role of Hubris

The founder was an extraordinarily talented engineer who had developed machines that were extremely productive, innovative and protected by more than 10 patents. Unfortunately, he could not accept that he needed to comply with even basic business practices and the law. His hubris prevented the company from operating profitably even though it had capabilities unlike any other in the world at the time. Even before he got into financial trouble he ignored the law, lied to authorities to raise money and allowed an associate in Los Angeles to profit through fraudulent misrepresentations and falsified MSG contracts.

Ultimately, his hubris caused his personal bankruptcy and the loss of his family's house and livelihood. None of it needed to happen.

Chapter 2
Operation Target Drone

"There's something wrong if you're always right."

- A. H. Glasgow

Background

Michael had an advanced degree from Harvard and worked as a senior product analyst for a very successful computer company. His research led him to conclude that the advances in microchips would render all cash registers in the world obsolete within a few years. He reasoned that the registers in use then were based on costly and highly inflexible electromechanical technology which would be superseded by semiconductor technology. In fact, within two years of starting his new company, NCR, the world's largest competitor and the then dominant manufacturer of electromechanical cash registers, wrote off $50 million of its manufacturing plant and inventory assets because they were all based on the future of electromechanical cash registers.

Michael's new company did business through 250 cash register dealers across the United States and a direct salesforce of about 10 individuals who called on major retail accounts. Each time a major account was assigned to the corporate salesforce, the dealer received an agreement which gave the dealer a percentage of all revenues from that “major” account for many years.

Position

I became vice president of product marketing and had responsibility for product lifecycle from inception through development and ultimately through the replacement by new products. The company was split into three major product areas: grocery, general merchandise retailing and hospitality. In the early 1980s the three largest customers were Walmart, Walgreens and Safeway.

A couple of years into my time with the company I was also given responsibility for coordinating all the service activities not done by the dealerships. Most of the dealerships were small companies most often created by a salesperson and a service person from one of the large cash register companies. Their business model was based on providing sales and service for the cash register manufacturers. Service was only provided during the dealership’s normal business hours. As a result, most of the dealerships did not provide service at night or on the weekends.

Events

The company was wildly successful. For example, in its first full year on the NYSE it was the top performing stock as measured by the percentage of increase in the share value from January 1st to December 31st. Unfortunately, at the end of the next year it was declared by a prominent business magazine to be "one of the 10 worst run New York Stock Exchange companies."

During the five years that I worked there, I always reported to Michael, the CEO. During that time, we acquired at least 10 companies in Europe (often the largest distributor in each country) and Michael had each of the country managers continue to report directly to him; a clear sign that hubris was at play. In fact, at the time that the company finally collapsed, Michael had 23 direct reports. As one of them I can confirm that it was extremely difficult to get any time with him to discuss important business issues. He believed that he could manage these executives better than anyone else and perhaps he could have, just not all at the same time.

A second example of Michael's hubris was reflected in a discussion we had related to the hotel and motel products. The dealership service organizations were generally providing services only during the week and often not after 6 PM. The hotel/motel product line required service to support customers during the critical night balancing efforts most often done between midnight and 2 AM. This process reconciles the rooms that are occupied with the guest portfolios and revenue. Unfortunately, this was a gross mismatch for the dealership organizations that had no service between 6 PM and 8 AM or on the weekends. Our business in this sector had started off successfully because the value proposition provided by electronic cash registers as opposed to mechanical cash registers was substantial. For example, the registers could contain a list of the rooms and therefore the long-standing requirement to manually develop and put room folders into a paper tub file was not necessary. Unfortunately, many of our customers grew to hate us because of problems associated with getting service during their critical night closings. It became clear we could not service the registers through the dealer organization and a significant number of customers began sending registers back and threatening legal actions for business disruptions and lack of support.

Based on a series of personal discussions both directly with customers and indirectly with the dealer organization, I went to Michael and suggested that we get out of the hotel/motel business because of the clear disconnect between the requirements for night balancing and the lack of service through the dealer organization. Furthermore, we were losing money in that business because our sales were declining when the dealer organization recognized that they could not service these customers. There were also problems with the technical capabilities of the registers. For example, in a hotel or motel that had more than 50 rooms there would have to be multiple registers but at that point, the technology did not allow the registers to access each other's customer sets. The result was that during the checkout operation separate lines had to be formed for customers that were checking out on separate registers. This meant that in a busy checkout time there could be four people in line waiting for one register with no one in the other line. This was very difficult to explain to unhappy customers that saw one register idle and the other register backed up and causing a substantial wait time.

Despite the overwhelming evidence for eliminating this product line or trying to find a buyer for it, Michael's decision was that we continue the line, which we did, to growing customer dissatisfaction and legal actions by both dealerships and customers.

A third example of Michael's hubris involves the payment of commissions to the major accounts salespeople. Of the more than 10 individuals in the major accounts sales organization, three were superior performers. One managed Walgreens, one managed Walmart and one managed Safeway. The company was doing extremely well in meeting their requirements through the efforts of these three superior performers. In mid-to-late September of one year, Michael calculated the potential commissions for these three individuals based on their run-rates and backlogs and realized that they were on a path to earn more than he did as CEO in that fiscal year. This caused him so much distress that he then invoked a clause in the commission structure agreement that allowed him to change it and then capped the commissions for that year at about the amounts they had already earned. This meant that almost none of the sales they recorded in the fourth quarter of that fiscal year would be commissionable. Not surprisingly all three were extremely highly motivated by their earnings; one of the most important ingredients of successful salespeople.

Several of us on Michael's executive staff, especially the Senior Vice President of Sales and

I, strongly suggested that he not do this. He rejected the idea that putting a cap on the commissions for these three individuals would in fact affect fourth-quarter sales to those three companies. (Those of us that had dealt directly with the three individuals and three companies involved knew that each of the individuals had very strong personal and candid relationships with the buying organizations. I spoke with one of the individuals affected and after he received the news, he made a sales call and requested that his customer suspend all orders except for emergency requirements until the beginning of the following year. They, like the other two companies, complied with the major account sales person's request. The company missed its fourth-quarter revenue targets by a number roughly equal to the lost revenue from these three companies. Not at all surprising was the fact that the three salesmen involved had terrific first quarters in the following year.

A fourth example of Michael's entrepreneurial hubris led to my conclusion that an entrepreneur often has difficulty differentiating between an idea and the physical implementation of that idea. On many occasions, I have, perhaps, humorously called this a "genetic defect." In fact, it may be a very important driver of the creative process which has led to so many successes.

At an annual dealers' conference Michael began to talk about a new product concept based on a minicomputer which would be developed and available for selling to small department stores. After describing the potential product and setting the price at $40,000 from the podium,

Michael began taking orders for the product from the dealers in the banquet hall. He was able to successfully describe the role the product could play in dealership finances to such an extent that well over 200 orders were taken in less than 30 minutes. He told the dealers that the company could deliver in six to nine months.

After this speech and sales effort, I went to him and pointed out that the company did not even have the first word on paper describing the system that he had just been selling. My responsibility was not only to design the product but also to build it, test it and develop all supporting documentation for successfully installing it. When I told Michael that we hadn't even started the specification of the requirements, he responded so forcefully that I believed that somewhere in his head, it was already done.

Results

Several months later I toured the country for an initiative I created, which became known internally as "Operation Target Drone." The purpose of this initiative was to allow the dealers to come to a meeting in each of five cities and express their total dissatisfaction with our inability to deliver the department store system and to give them a new schedule. It was only mildly successful, and most orders were ultimately cancelled.

To get a low price for the retail system described above, the entrepreneur made a huge commitment to a hardware company to purchase several thousand computers. The agreement with the hardware company was very simple: if the company met its volume purchasing requirements, the machines were heavily discounted (60-80%). However, if the company over the period of two years did not meet its volume requirements it would then have to pay back the entire unearned discount based on its actual purchases. During this time the company was building a new corporate headquarters. When the computer company calculated the amount of the unearned discount it was so large that the corporate headquarters was transferred to the computer company as partial payment of the unearned discount. Within a year the CEO entrepreneur was replaced by the board, the company was put up for sale and the company was delisted by the NYSE.

The stock had hit an all-time high in the range of $60 a share, but the company was eventually sold at a share price of about $4. Shareholders lost hundreds of millions of dollars and Michael became a member of the "90+% CEO Club." I give this dubious distinction to those CEOs that have eroded their public company's market capitalization by greater than 90%.

The Role of Hubris

The entrepreneur got many things right. His understanding of the state of retail automation and the industry's total reliance on electromechanical cash registers was brilliant. However, his hubris did not allow him to tolerate the notion that he might be wrong on some important aspects of the business. The company's failure did not need to happen.

Chapter 3
But It Is Not in the "Use of Funds" Statement

"Do not look where you fell, but where you slipped."

- Liberian proverb

Background

Gary was a brilliant software engineer who created a very new and innovative way of developing business applications. He licensed his initial software to a large company on a royalty basis, was immensely successful and was still receiving royalty payments 20 years later. He crafted a new vision for a software development tool for web applications that would be a disruptive improvement in both the time and cost to create them.

Position

He started a new company to produce this new tool and I was recruited as its CEO.

Events

We put together a business plan and secured $4 million in funding which allowed us to proceed with the development of the new system based on Java and Enterprise Java Beans. Early development was immensely successful. Unfortunately, within eight weeks of finalizing the investment round, he presented me and the company with a demand for about $2 million. Honoring it would severely limit the business, marketing and development plans. The document soliciting the $4 million investment included a "Use of Funds" section but it did not include any payment of funds to the founder. I refused to authorize the payment without an opinion from the legal counsel who structured the deal and prepared the term sheet. It happened that the law firm was also an investor in the round and I believed that they would agree that the payment was not justified and therefore should not be made.

Results

Unfortunately, I was wrong and the law firm approved the payment. The development plans were severely slowed because the anticipated development staff was cut by half and the product was never built. As a side note, the law firm which had invested $100,000 of the $4 million round subsequently declared insolvency.

The Role of Hubris ... or was it just greed

The entrepreneur was totally correct in the concept and design for the new product. Early beta tests proved that web applications could be successfully developed in days rather than months. Working prototypes were created for both FTD and Kelly Services. Hubris came into play when he decided to take funds from the equity raised with the belief that the product could be developed without regard to the detailed development plan he and I created together and which was provided in the business plan. The brilliant and innovative web application development tool was never built.

Chapter 4

Gun-jumping and Obstruction of Justice

"Power intoxicates men. It is never voluntarily surrendered. It must be taken from them."

- J. F. Byrnes

Background

Gemstar–TV Guide was a result of a merger after the courts sustained an assertion that TV Guide had infringed on the Gemstar patent portfolio. Henry Yuen was the founder and CEO of Gemstar. He has a Ph.D. in applied mathematics from Caltech. He taught at Caltech and at New

York University, and then obtained a law degree from Loyola Law School.

Henry founded Gemstar in 1986 and began licensing the patent for a mathematically elegant way of allowing a five-digit numeric code to be inputted into specially engineered television recording devices which allowed them to accurately schedule recordings. TV Guide published that code for all its programs in its weekly magazine. Gemstar sued asserting infringement. It eventually prevailed and forced TV Guide to merge with Gemstar as part of the settlement. According to Henry the major shareholders of TV Guide agreed to give Henry voting rights over their shares for a period of five years.

Henry left Gemstar in 2003, after the company revealed manipulation of revenue and other accounting problems. He was convicted of securities fraud in 2006 and ordered to pay $22 million in penalties. As of April 25, 2007, his whereabouts were unknown and he was declared a "fugitive from justice."

[Sidebar: Elsie Leung served as the company's CFO. She and Henry resigned at the same time and became co-plaintiffs in an eventual suit to recover their severance payments. A portion of the opinion by the 9th District Court is shown as Appendix B as a way of demonstrating the role that hubris played in the down fall of Gemstar-TV Guide.]

Position

I was hired as a senior vice president in 2000 and reported to Henry with a dotted line to Elsie, the CFO. My primary responsibilities included managing infra-structure and special projects for Henry. The infrastructure was extensive and complex and included the technology to collect TV Guide program data and then download it to regional TV Guide printing centers across the country. In order to meet the printing center time schedules, the infrastructure was especially demanding. I was also responsible for the technology that uploaded electronic program guides (EPG) to the television set's program display channel. In general, the professionals in the company that reported into my organization were both dedicated and competent.

Events

There are two situations that stand out which reflect Henry's hubris and perhaps his less than honorable motives. First, he and Elsie rejected a proposal by the chief accounting officer and me to combine several accounting systems into one. We felt that this would significantly reduce the workload related to preparing SEC reports and make the reports available more quickly.

Subsequently we learned that the company was using one company to purchase advertising from another company thereby increasing its revenues at a very high percentage. These increases were used as proof that the new company was extremely successful.

Second, during staff meetings he and Elsie would often begin speaking Chinese to each other totally removing the rest of us from the conversation, deliberations and collaboration.

Results

The results of Henry's hubris are far too many and lengthy to cover here but some are covered below.

All references in this section (A1 through A11) are included in Appendix A.

In July of 2000, an article was published: "Massive new company could dominate EPG market." It pointed out that TV Guide and Gemstar had been given the go-ahead to merge by the Department of Justice creating an electronic programming guide (EPG) company. It also announced that Henry would serve as chairman and CEO. The $9.2 billion stock and debt deal gave Gemstar shareholders 55% of the combined company. (A1)

In February 2003, the Justice Department reached a settlement with the new company related to premerger coordination which is illegal under federal law. Premerger coordination, often called "gun-jumping," involves practices wherein the two organizations agree to stop competing for customers and coordinating pricing and terms. It is a violation of the Hart-Scott-Rodino Act of 1976. Gun-jumping also violates Section 1 of the Sherman Act. The Justice Department obtained the largest civil penalty in its history for these actions. The penalties were $5.67 million, and an injunction was also issued as part of the consent decree to give customers who signed contracts with Gemstar-TV Guide during the premerger period a chance to rescind those contracts. (A2)

In September of 2005 it was reported that Henry would plead guilty to obstructing a Securities and Exchange Commission investigation into alleged accounting irregularities at Gemstar-TV Guide from 1999 to 2002. The plea agreement from the U.S. attorney's office said that Henry would serve six months of home detention during a two-year period of probation. He was also required to contribute $1 million to charities representing low-income victims of fraud and to pay a $250,000 fine. (A3)

However, the U.S. SEC openly criticized the Justice Department's plea agreement telling the judge that prosecutors may have been "too lenient" in settling the case. In response, the judge delayed the approval of the plea deal. (A4).

In March of 2006, a federal judge found that Henry was liable for securities fraud which involved inflating the company's revenues by $248 million to increase its stock value. The federal judge also found Henry liable for misrepresenting facts to the company's auditors and falsifying its books. (A5)

A few months later, in May of 2006, Henry was ordered by the SEC to pay $22 million for his role in the accounting fraud. In addition, Henry was permanently barred from serving as an officer or director of any public company. The court found that Henry received $10.6 million in ill-gotten gains consisting of $3 million in gross bonus compensation during the period of the fraud and $7.6 million in excess trading profits he received by selling Gemstar-TV Guide stock during the period of the fraud. The SEC's Pacific Regional Director is quoted as saying, "The final judgment and the permanent bar against future service as an officer or director reflect the seriousness of Mr. Yuen's misconduct and the vital importance of punishing and deterring securities law violations which harm the investing public." (A6)

May of 2008 was a pretty exciting time for Henry as the following summary will show.

In May of 2008, he was indicted on a felony charge of obstructing an SEC investigation into Gemstar-TV Guide's alleged accounting irregularities. It pointed out that Henry was among those subpoenaed which required him to provide several items including handwritten, typed or electronic correspondence. The subpoena included documents on Henry's computer but according to the indictment after Henry received his subpoena, he deleted emails and Gemstar corporate documents from the device. The rumor circulating at the time was that Henry had taken the computer home and run "off the shelf" disc scrambling software to make the documents irretrievable. Subsequently, the FBI executed a search warrant, recovered the computer, unscrambled the information on the hard drive and secured all the relevant documents.

What is not clear is whether Henry will ever answer to the charges because as of May 2008, he had disappeared and the federal government was asking anybody who knew of his whereabouts to contact the FBI in Los Angeles. (A7)

Also, in May of 2008, he was charged by the Justice Department with obstructing an investigation. It was a felony count that referred to obstructing an SEC probe of the alleged irregularities at Gemstar from 1999 through 2002. At this time, it was also reported that two years earlier, a federal judge in Los Angeles found Henry liable for securities fraud by inflating sales from 1999 to 2002. Henry was ordered to pay $22.3 million in fines and forfeitures.

It was also reported that in a hearing in 2007, the SEC lawyer said that Henry had made no effort to pay the judgment against him and had about $150 million in assets outside the U.S. (A8)

Also, in May of 2008, the Securities and Exchange Commission released a statement referring to "Litigation Release Number 20599" which confirmed its interests and conclusions in the above issues. (A9)

In May of 2008, a U.S. attorney spokesperson said, "We don't know where he is right now. And by now, he should be aware of the charges against him." Henry had failed to pay the $22.3 million in fines and penalties from his previous conviction. That judgment was affirmed by the 9th U.S. Circuit Court of Appeals in April. Appendix B includes excerpts from that proceeding. It was also reported at that time, that the SEC had been unable to seize Henry's assets and claimed in an earlier filing that Henry gave $42 million to third parties and moved substantial amounts of cash offshore to evade seizure of assets. Given all the data related to Henry and his hubris, it is interesting to note that the SEC senior trial counsel said that he expected Henry to pay eventually. "We fully expect that now that the Ninth Circuit has ruled, Mr. Yuen will honor the judgment." (A10) Some of us who knew the situation, suspected that he was overly optimistic about Henry's eventual compliance.

Also, in May of 2008 Henry was declared a "fugitive from justice" because he did not turn himself in to authorities after being charged with obstruction of justice by the U.S. Attorney in Los Angeles. It was reported that a spokesman said, "The ex-CEO's apparent flight from justice and failure to pay $22.3 million in fines for securities fraud, lying to auditors and falsifying Gemstar's books to inflate the company's revenues by $248 million from 2000 to 2002 comes as an unwelcomed reminder of the woes that have afflicted Gemstar-TV Guide which was acquired by Macrovision on March 2nd for $2.3 billion." (A11)

The Role of Hubris

Henry's hubris was so profound that it affected almost all of what he did. Phrases like "what was he thinking" and "that was just stupid" are not appropriate. Henry was extremely bright (e.g., Ph.D. from Caltech and law degree from Loyola) and could never be considered anything but brilliant. Therefore, his behaviors need to be viewed as qualitatively different from using his intelligence. In fact, some of his decisions highlight the extent of his hubris: the use of off-the-shelf software to scramble data on his hard drive after he received the FBI subpoena and then keeping the computer and its drive at his house. Any rational person would have believed that the FBI forensic computing labs were smart enough to determine what had been done with the scrambling software and then undo it. This is apparently what happened.

Also, the example of his collusion with TV Guide during the premerger talks is another example of his hubris. As an attorney it is reasonable to assume he knew this to be highly illegal.

Henry goes down in history as part of the "90+% CEO Club" (CEOs that have eroded their market capitalization by at least 90%). In fairness to Henry, it went up substantially in response to his and Elsie's manipulation of revenues so maybe he may only be a member of the "50+% Club."

Chapter 5
Billions of Dollars of Wealth Creation without Hubris

"Every morning I wake up committed to helping great people do great things."

- Jerre Stead

Acceptance Speech - National Association of Corporate Boards Lifetime Achievement Award, November 2017

Background

I first met Jerre Stead in 1993 when he took over NCR after it was purchased by AT&T. At that time, I was chief technology officer at Kmart and NCR was one of our major vendors. Kmart was also one of NCR's major customers and a very desirable customer because of the substantial budget to bring Kmart into a more automated technology environment. In more than 25 years, I have never known Jerre to demonstrate even the slightest hint of hubris.

What makes this story even better is that during the time I have known Jerre, he has helped companies increase shareholder wealth by more than $10 billion. This is in clear contrast to most of the other stories in this book.

It confirms that not only does entrepreneurial hubris often kill companies; the total lack of hubris can contribute to profound long-term increases in stakeholder value.

Events

During the five years that Jerre and I worked together at IHS, we acquired a new company on average every 6½ weeks. When an acquisition target was identified, all company organizations were mobilized to conduct due diligence for their areas. Although sometimes the timeframe was shortened, the processes surrounding due diligence for these acquisition targets were generally the same. After all organizations completed their due diligence, the senior officers and their reports who were responsible for presenting the results were gathered physically and by conference call with Jerre. Never once in these meetings was he heavy-handed with the presenters. It was always very clear that he was attending so that he could learn as much as possible before deciding. After these due diligence "readouts," Jerre made the final decision as to whether the acquisition would be presented to the board of directors.

Results

During this five-year period, IHS more than doubled in both sales and profitability.

The Role of Hubris

In all the years that I have known Jerre, he has never exhibited anything close to the dys-functional characteristics described as hubris in this book.

There is, however, an interesting distinction that should be made between leadership born of hubris and leadership born of competence. Prior to working for Jerre at IHS, I worked for him at Ingram Micro. At one of the first meetings of the executive team at Ingram Micro, there was an extensive debate about some aspect of employee remuneration including levels of stock options to be granted upon certain milestones in corporate results. One of my colleagues made the huge mistake of telling the group that he felt that we were "close to consensus." Some of us who knew Jerre knew that the use of the 'C' word was every bit as inflammatory as dropping the 'F' bomb. We knew there would be an explosion; we just didn't know how big it would be. Because the colleague that had used the 'consensus' word was new to the organization, Jerre was direct and forceful but not agitated. Jerre's message was a very simple one. Organizations that move forward based on consensus do so only by extracting the lowest common denominator of agreement and performance objectives. He strongly encouraged my new colleague to never use the 'consensus' word again.

Jerre's approach always depended on a different 'C' word: collaboration. He encouraged collaboration among individuals and business groups across the company. They were an important part of making an informed quality decision. In the end, he made the decision and therefore was accountable for it.

The extraordinary success of Jerre's career had everything to do with his commitment to collaboration, his informed decisions and accountability, flawless execution and absolutely nothing to do with hubris.

Chapter 6
He Was a CPA

"If you wish to know what a man is, place him in authority."

- Yugoslav proverb

Background

Paul created a company that served its customers by identifying environmental and health standards, placing them in a large database and making them available through software and subscriptions. A very large company with revenues in the range of $1 billion purchased this product and the database in two stages. The first stage gave the acquiring company the opportunity to exclusively market the database and software for which it paid $4 million. The second stage was a complete acquisition of the database and supporting software for which Paul's company was paid an additional $11 million.

Paul decided to create a replacement for the software and database he had just sold and asked me to run it. One of the employees of the old company who transferred to the new company was a bookkeeper who managed the company's bank accounts.

Position

I took the position of CEO after the founder assured me that we had a little over $4 million with which to build a new platform, a new architecture and bring on new staff and third-party relationships to populate the database and keep it updated.

Events

Within 90 days, these plans were in motion with a new CFO, a new head of sales, a new major account sales person and a new head of content acquisition. The bookkeeper reported to the new CFO but, as I found out later, still had very strong ties to the founder.

A few months after the new staff was in place and the new development was launched, the CFO and I had an amazing conversation. He alerted me that rather than having funds consistent with the $4 million initial founder commitment, our cash balance had gone down to about $2 million, half of what it was supposed to be. When I asked him how this was possible he said that the founder had used his friendly and loyal bookkeeper to transfer well over $1.5 million to other companies, to personal accounts and to pay off personal credit cards. In fact, the amount transferred to pay off personal credit cards was in the range of $10,000 a week for the last few months. When I asked the CFO whether there was documentation that would qualify them as corporate expenses, the CFO said there was not. I then said that the founder, who was a CPA, should know better than to receive reimbursements without documentation. The

CFO then made one of the most memorable statements in all my experience. He said, "Well, he used to be a CPA." I then asked what he meant by that and he said that the founder's CPA license had been revoked by the State of California when he pleaded guilty to eight felony counts of federal fraud. (It is common for companies to ask potential employees if they've ever been convicted of a felony but rarely if ever do potential employees ask management if they have been convicted of a felony ... and I had not.)

Results

It became clear that the financial plans which were to create a new infrastructure architecture, new software and a new database were in jeopardy. Because of the founder's felony conviction, he could not hold stock, so his portion of the stock was held by his wife. But he also controlled her stock, and, through influence, most of the other shareholders and the board.

I began to plan for securing a bridge loan so that we could continue the strategic plan to produce a new hardware architecture, new software and a new database. I presented a plan to the founder under which we would raise $500,000 as a bridge loan with conversion rights to a new equity round which we knew would significantly dilute existing shareholders. The founder believed that he could make the company successful without funding and would not support this approach, so I resigned. The company failed.

The Role of Hubris

This founder, like many other examples, was very successful for many years. Unfortunately, the founder's unwillingness to recognize that there were moral, ethical and legal issues with which he had to deal led to the failure of the company and the resulting loss of several million dollars of invested capital and the jobs of about 40 people. Once again, a great idea was sabotaged by a founder's hubris.

Chapter 7
$17 Million Pre-Money? ... Really?

"Oh Lord, grant that we may always be right, for Thou knowest we will never change our minds."

- Scottish prayer

Background

The entrepreneur, Don, pointed out to a mutual acquaintance, Jeff, that car titles were being processed the same way as they had been processed 100 years ago - totally dependent on paperwork. The concept that we began to develop was to create a new technology environment including an authenticating server which would electronically hold all valid titles so there was a single electronic "source of truth." With this new platform, all activities related to car titles would be far easier to execute and expenses could be reduced by at least 90%. In fact, when a vehicle was sold under the existing system a signature of the owner or representative of the owner would be applied to the document and then the document physically moved to the new owner. As an example, a large vehicle leasing organization had recently sold a fleet of cars and an individual representative had to sign thousands of titles. Titles were kept in very large warehouses and had to be indexed and accessed each time the vehicle changed ownership.

Position

I agreed to act as a consultant to this project and put a very substantial amount of time into it. There were four of us involved: Don, Jeff, the attorney and me. I took the responsibility for identifying several “use cases,” supporting processes and the technical architecture that would allow them to be executed.

Events

When I met with the entrepreneur through Jeff he said that he was looking for a $17 million pre-money valuation for his idea. This number was so outrageous that Jeff and I rejected it immediately. However, the concept that he was describing seemed to have substantial value if we could sign an initial customer or two and then get a prototype built. I produced detailed process diagrams showing how the system would work with several important use cases and how the solution would be architected. The entrepreneur, Jeff and I, and an attorney got together and reviewed the general outline of the processes and the infrastructure that I had put together. We agreed that this work provided appropriate first steps.

Jeff and I met to discuss initial customer possibilities. Jeff had an extremely close relationship with a decision-maker that would agree to install a prototype. The entrepreneur, Jeff and I then met with a software firm that could be used to develop the prototype. We had total alignment on the way the system would work, the architecture, an initial customer and a developer that would charge us less than

$100,000 for a working prototype. With these ingredients, we could have had an initial customer who would process about 500 titles a month and could be up and running within four months.

Results

When we began to look at developing a business plan that would allow us to raise money to build the prototype, the issue of pre-money valuation came up again. Unfortunately, the entrepreneur refused to budge from his exorbitant pre-money valuation and the project was abandoned and still has not been pursued.

The Role of Hubris

The entrepreneur felt so strongly that his concept was of and by itself worth so many millions of dollars that he was not willing to consider a substantially lower valuation which would have allowed startup funding, so a prototype could be developed and installed. The concept may have been a billion-dollar idea, but the hubris of the entrepreneur prevented the prototype to be built and the first customer to be secured. The problem continues to be unsolved. Jeff, the attorney and I never recovered any of our invested time or energy and the entrepreneur's ideas have produced no value.

Chapter 8
Beacons, Beacons and More Beacons

"Hear the other side."

- St. Augustine

Background

An acquaintance was operating as an interim financial advisor to a company that was about one year old. He asked me to meet with the founder/entrepreneur as part of his due diligence. The entrepreneur, Barbara, designed and engineered a very inexpensive device (she called a "beacon") that could communicate with an application on a smart phone. The business concept was: install these beacons in high-end restaurants and bars so that customers coming into the restaurant who had installed and activated an application on the smart phone would be sent messages from that restaurant related to menu items and special offers. The beacons required robust wireless connectivity to a server in the facility. By placing beacons in the restaurant and bar entrances, communications with customers could take place in real time.

Position

With my background in facility technology, I was asked to help conduct due diligence prior to significant funding by a venture organization.

Events

In a meeting, the entrepreneur laid out the overall architecture of the solution. It had five major components: beacons, a server communicating with them in the facility, software to run on the server to manage the interactions between the beacons and any smart phone, software to be downloaded onto a smart phone and a Wi-Fi network to connect the beacons with the server and the customers' smart phones.

The entrepreneur's focus was dominated with the design and development of the beacons without much regard for the remaining four elements of the solution architecture.

In a subsequent and lengthy meeting where the five elements were reviewed and potential budgets were developed, it was clear that only the beacons had been subjected to a serious analysis. We asked the entrepreneur about the amount of research completed to determine how many bars and restaurants had Wi-Fi that could be used for public smart phone access. She was unable to cite any data other than the single restaurant that had agreed to help her launch an installation because of her personal relationship with the owner.

Results

It was clear after a long four-hour meeting that the technology solution which was dependent on public Wi-Fi availability had not been analyzed adequately. It was also clear that the fundamental business proposition was flawed. The solution required the software to be downloaded prior to a customer entering the bar or restaurant and activating the software before or when entering. This meant that the solution required many customers to search the application portfolio for their smart phone, download the application and activate it prior to entering the bar or restaurant. The entrepreneur's defense of this potential flaw was that when there were hundreds of her installations, customers would routinely activate the application upon entering an establishment.

With the issues raised, the recommendation to the venture fund was to pass on the investment. Subsequently, the company continued to spend its limited resources on the design and manufacturing of additional beacons. However, the solution never had an initial installation and the company failed within several months.

The business model may well have been flawed but it never had a chance given the opinion of the entrepreneur that public Wi-Fi services operated in many bars and restaurants at that time. She was wrong but refused to subject her error to subsequent analysis and data.

The Role of Hubris

The entrepreneur could not tolerate the idea that most bars and restaurants did not have public Wi-Fi available. Therefore, the architecture of the solution would fail even if the underlying concept was viable. That the solution might have been successful with a variant of the idea was never fully explored due to entrepreneurial hubris.

Chapter 9

The Company Is in Trouble and I Need Help

"An army of 1,000 is easy to find, but, ah, how hard to find a general."

- Chinese proverb

Background

Two years after Silver Lake Partners and other investors completed taking Seagate Technology private, the company spun off its Removable Storage Solutions division. Howard Matthews came into the newly spun off organization and took over as the CEO and general manager. Even though the company had been in operation, it did not have the strategic, operational and cultural separation needed to be a successful free-standing company.

According to T.C. Doyle, in a CRN article published in May of 2004, Howard's job was "building a startup from the remnants of a $225 million division of Seagate." Howard's task included building, leading and motivating a new team to leave an admittedly comfortable operating arrangement which allowed the company to utilize Seagate's ERP, HR resources, finance and other critical processes. He also had to battle the Seagate corporate staff that wanted to continue to provide services at high costs based on their assumption that a new and competent team could not be built fast enough to run a successful company. In April of 2003, the company changed its name to Certance and in October, 2004, it executed a highly successful sale relative to the investors' expectations when Quantum Corporation acquired Certance for over $100 million. The acquisition was completed in 2005.

Position

In early 2003, I was asked to help Howard when the company encountered a major problem with its technology conversion to a new and separate Oracle system.

Events

As part of the spinoff from Seagate Technology, the new company was required to install its own ERP and no longer be dependent upon Seagate's Oracle system. The cutover from the Seagate Oracle system to a new Oracle system occurred in January of 2003. The need for new technology leadership was prompted by the resignation of the previous head of technology, a former Seagate executive, when the cutover occurred.

In early discussions with Howard it became clear that the failures of the new Oracle environment were having a devastating effect on the company; especially on its ability to ship products to depots in Asia and then to fulfill a steady stream of orders from several large manufacturers including IBM and HP. In fact, in the first three weeks of January not a single delivery was made to any of the strategic partners.

Results

Howard and I met nearly every day in January and early February; he supported the creation of a task force to address the severe logistical issues caused by the new Oracle environment. This task force met at 5 PM Pacific Time every business day to allow the participation of associates who worked in the Asia manufacturing facility in Penang, Malaysia to be on the call. Howard's very active and committed leadership for all the necessary initiatives allowed the company to correct the issues. As a result, there were no unshipped orders by the end of the first quarter and the company revenues hit first quarter targets.

Howard told me that when the company was spun off from Seagate it had been losing money and had negative cash flow. The result was the valuation at the time of the spin off was set to zero. Howard's entrepreneurial focus and his ability to restructure the company and hire the right people resulted in the sale to Quantum Corporation in 2005.

As a side note, even though members of the executive leadership team had not been with the company long enough for vesting of their options, Howard, as part of the acquisition agreement with Quantum, insisted that all options immediately vest and be honored.

The Role of Hubris

One of Howard's great strengths as a senior executive was to "know what he did not know." This strength and its successful implementation are the absolute opposite of hubris.

Chapter 10

They Are the Same Cost ... and Don't Ask Me Again

"To accept good advice is but to increase one's own ability."

- Johan Wolfgang von Goethe

Background

A firm that specialized in long-range facial recognition successfully demonstrated technology that could identify individuals contained in a data base at 200 meters. The company received several million dollars in government funding and there was great interest in moving the technology to 250 meters and beyond. There also was some interest in nonmilitary use primarily with county and state law enforcement agencies. The company had previously demonstrated very successful technology for facial recognition on a smaller and less complicated device at 75 meters.

Position

I was asked to join the company as CEO and work with the founder to productize both devices. One of the police agencies that had expressed an interest was a county sheriff's department in a southern state that was known for its early adoption and development of technology. The department had a history of receiving substantial federal government funding for its efforts.

Events

The county sheriff's department with which we were working requested a proposal that would allow them to acquire and test five of the longer-range devices. Up to that point, there were only three prototypes, but the proposal required that the company have definitive information on pricing and delivery dates for the devices. This meant that the company needed to develop manufacturing documentation so potential manufacturing organizations could bid on making preproduction prototypes to meet the requirements of the county sheriff's proposal. The shorter-range technology was called the B75 and the longer-range technology was called the B200. Both interacted wirelessly with laptops that could be deployed in the field using battery power.

When the founder was asked how much funding would be required to develop manufacturing documentation for the B75 his response was one year and $1.5 million. When he was asked for an estimate of how much funding would be required to develop manufacturing documentation for the B200, his answer was the same. It was clear from simply looking at the two devices that the B200 was three times heavier and included far more parts than the B75. It was clear that the same estimate could not be accurate for both. The company that had produced the prototypes had an engineering and development facility in southern California. I suggested to the founder that he and I take both devices down to the facility to meet with the head of engineering. The round trip to the manufacturing and engineering facility could easily be done within a single day.

The founder refused to schedule such a meeting and continued to insist that his answers to the manufacturing documentation funding question were accurate. In the meantime, the due date for the proposal to the county sheriff's department was getting close and there were two remaining questions that had to be answered before it was submitted: first, how much time it would take to develop the manufacturing documentation and, second, how much the B200 would cost to be manufactured based on that manufacturing documentation. I showed one of the prototypes of the B75 to a friend who manufactured sophisticated technology equipment for the United States Marines and his estimate for developing manufacturing documentation was in the range of three months and $100,000. This was far less than the founder's estimate. The entrepreneur held firmly that his estimates were accurate and became increasingly hostile when I pointed out that the same estimate for both devices was totally illogical.

There was a bright spot in this environment. I had an opportunity to work with one of the best financial executives ever. Fred not only developed pro forma analyses and projections for the business but added tremendous savvy to discussions on how to move forward. Along the way he pointed out that the company had raised more than $2 million in venture funding. Some funding came from an individual who knew the father of the founder but had no personal relationship with the founder himself. This led to an awkward confrontation described below.

Results

The proposal to the county sheriff's department was submitted without details about the delivery schedule for the prototypes or the eventual cost. After my leaving the company, an arrangement was made with the department to use prototypes for an initial implementation. The results were unsuccessful.

An individual mentioned above had invested $100,000 due to a personal relationship with the entrepreneur's father. This individual passed away and in his estate were the company shares that he purchased. In its attempt to settle the estate, his family wanted an evaluation so they could determine the value of the shares. Unfortunately, there was none available. In fact, in all my conversations with the founder it became clear that he did not value the minority shareholders and the investments they had made. This attitude frustrated both myself and Fred. Included is Appendix C that provides a summary of common funding stages. Stage III is often overlooked and may be the most troublesome as a company matures or misses its targets. This is primarily because it places the early enthusiasm of the startup environment under scrutiny by "outsiders."

The Role of Hubris

The fact that the entrepreneur could not accept that he was clearly wrong on the time schedule and funding requirements for the manufacturing documentation for the two devices led to a total stalemate for the company. His lack of regard for minority shareholders also produced an environment that made any return on the shareholders' investment highly unlikely.

Chapter 11
I Can Save You $50 million a Year... Just Trust Me

"Charisma without character leads to catastrophe."

- Peter Kuzmich

Background

Chuck was an extremely good salesperson and was able to sell himself and his credibility like few others. However, part of his charisma was the ability to exaggerate his previous successes to the point of fabrication. Because of his ability to sell himself and his ideas, the potential customers with whom he engaged did not question his assertions. For example, he maintained that in a previous implementation of his processes and technology, he had saved about $2 million in direct product costs for a large medical center and helped it move from losing about $10 million a year to making about $50 million a year. His persuasive personality allowed these assertions to stand without serious analysis or scrutiny.

Position

When a major opportunity arose in southern California at one of the large medical centers, I was asked to assume the responsibility of managing West Coast operations. The intent was to install technology that allowed major savings in the supply chain for all products and materials purchased by the hospital, its branches and clinics. Because of substantial analysis, it became clear that the marketplace of hospital and healthcare logistics was ripe for automation and competitive acquisition strategies.

Events

In mid-2016 a major proposal was given to the medical center in southern California. Chuck's assertion of his successful experience and his previous successful implementation became a major ingredient in furthering the proposal.

There were also meetings with potential venture funders to secure resources for developing a new version of the technology installed at the first hospital.

Results

As I got closer and closer to the operations I asked the one question that no one wanted to hear or answer: "How much of the technology installed in the first site is still operating?" After several painful conversations the accurate answer came out: none. The potential new hospital never accepted the proposal and in more than a year since it was developed, no action occurred.

The Role of Hubris

As was often the case, the entrepreneur's fundamental idea was sound. Chuck's assessment that huge potential savings could be secured from improved processes and technology across the healthcare supply chain was profoundly correct. Unfortunately, his belief that he alone had the knowledge and resources to implement the solution caused the company to stagnate.

Chapter 12
My Super Power is Negotiating ... Among Many Others

"Teach thy tongue to say: 'I do not know.'"

- Hebrew proverb

Background

Craig created a business plan and presented it to a venture capital conference in southern California. The business plan was one of the best presented at the conference and as a result several people invested $50,000 in convertible notes. A few months later the notes were converted at a 20% premium resulting in the acquisition of shares of stock.

The business was based on the observation that many smaller fashion brands had not kept up with their larger competitors in e-commerce and fulfillment services. The business plan pointed out that the market for services was huge and growing. These fashion brands had lost a material number of brick and mortar stores and therefore had been losing sales to competitors with viable e-commerce presences, especially through arrangements with Amazon.

Craig's business model allowed potential customers to sign up for a small fee or monthly minimum with the company. The fashion brand and the company had incentives to rapidly increase sales. For handling the e-commerce website, the company anticipated charging the fashion brand approximately 20% of sales. The initial assumption was that the brands would be able to fulfill product based on orders received by the company's e-commerce.

This turned out to be a bad assumption and more than half of the fashion brands did not have the internal capabilities to send product directly to consumers. The company's model was modified to include order fulfillment with consigned inventory, thereby eliminating any investment in inventory. Transactions occurred through a method called "flash title" which gave the company title to the goods only long enough to sell them using a credit card. The company then found a third-party that would hold the consigned inventory and process the orders and send them to customers. The use of credit cards guaranteed that the company received its payments, because when the orders were completed, the purchase amounts were transferred into the company's accounts. Once a month the brands' portion would be paid out.

The early investments were made because investors felt that the market was very large and that the business model allowed a relatively pain-free entry into e-commerce by the fashion brands. This resulted in a solid business plan.

The company continued to operate several years without any notification to shareholders. Even not having heard from them in a long period of time, I was still interested in this business model (and what had happened to the value of my shares). I approached the company and volunteered to assist with issues as directed by the CEO. One indication that the entrepreneurial founders believed they were above and beyond the reasonable rules of ethics and the legal system is demonstrated by the following story.

During one attempt to raise venture funds, a potential investor organization was told that the company had 50 employees. In fact, the company employee count was closer to 25. The fund decided to visit the company as part of its due diligence process. In preparation for the visit, one of the entrepreneurial founders went to a temporary staffing organization and hired 25 people for the following morning. The staffing agency was told that each of these people should bring a laptop computer and be prepared to look busy all day. I found it particularly offensive that one of the principals went about bragging about this fabrication.

Position

I entered the situation as an advisor to the CEO and took on the assignment of interim chief financial officer. I served in this position for about eight months. During that time, the company lost several customers and was having a significant problem meeting its measures of service.

Events

Eventually, it became clear that the company needed another financial investment and pro forma financial statements were created by the CEO (without my input I am happy to say). An investment of approximately $3 million at a pre-money valuation was secured.

The CEO provided 'top down' financial projections. This technique would build new customers into the financial pro forma and sales forecasts without regard to the names of those potential customers. For example, in the third quarter of one year it was forecasted that the company would acquire two large customers, three medium customers, a small customer and an enterprise customer. Forecasted sales increases were built on these predictions, but historically, the company never actually attained the sales levels forecasted in this way.

Of note, the CEO lived about 50 miles from the company headquarters during this time. And, the company rented the second floor of an expensive rental unit at the rate of $5,000 a month. Eventually, the apartment was eliminated from the company's expenses. During my time with the company, the CEO was in the office only two to three days a week.

Additionally, even though the company was going through substantial changes, the CEO did not believe in producing and circulating an organization chart even after it was pointed out that ISO 90001 certification requires organizational charts to help ensure quality and accountability. There were frequent complaints that employees did not know to whom they reported or the full scope of their responsibilities. The CEO also did not believe in disclosing information about the state of the company or its plans except during very lengthy and rambling nonspecific projections about the future.

The Role of Hubris

Despite spending less than 30 hours a week in the office, Craig felt he could manage all operations better than anyone else (and perhaps he could have). The problem is of course a single person's competence is not scalable. When various executive and middle management individuals left the company, Craig had a plan. He would assume their duties on a short-term basis with the belief that he could do anything better than anyone else. On several occasions he acknowledged the possibility that he was not a very good CEO, but this never precluded him from operating as if he were whenever he determined the company's operations needed him.

The fact that the company had been in existence for more than six years, had been operating under the same business plan as when it started but had lost more than $8 million, never deterred him from the strongly held belief that he, and only he, could operate the company successfully; a classic case of hubris.

Chapter 13
A Market of 550,000 Isn't Enough

"Nothing undermines openness more surely than certainty. Once we feel as if we have 'the answer,' all motivation to question our thinking disappears."

- Peter Seng

Background

Vince is a brilliant software engineer who had a vision of providing a software layer for legacy computing systems that would allow legacy machines to communicate with the Internet and mobile devices without changes to existing applications. He asserted that he spent $2 million of his own money developing the software.

Position

I was asked to help him as an interim CEO.

Events

The overall market was enormous and growing. It became clear that the single opportunity with the most potential was the more than 550,000 IBM AS/400s still in operation. The AS/400 introduced in the mid-1980s was an extremely successful minicomputer with a unique development language which included code supporting an integrated database architecture.

This integrated environment was part of the value proposition that the IBM AS/400 represented. However, it also meant that any major enhancements to applications operating on this platform would require major rewrites or even replacements without the kind of software layer that Vince had developed.

There was an extensive discussion about how to price such a valuable software platform. The final pricing scheme included a combination of per user licenses, per server licenses, and enterprise licenses.

Results

A previous organization with which I had worked had an AS/400 that was more than 20 years old and had about 30 users. I proposed to Vince that we calculate the list price using our new pricing schema and offer the potential customer a substantial discount. This would give us an initial installation into a friendly environment. He totally rejected that concept with the phrase "they are a billion-dollar company and they can afford to pay list." I pointed out that in all the time I had known the company, I never heard anyone express any dissatisfaction with the AS/400. But I also felt strongly that a sales presentation could be made that identified major opportunities within the AS/400 environment with Vince's new layer of software that allowed Internet access and mobile device utilization. He held firm to the notion that pricing should not be discounted so the presentation was never made.

It has now been several years since a fully functional environment for the AS/400 was available and demonstrated in two separate and remote test environments. There have been no sales or installations of this extremely valuable software primarily due to the entrepreneur's unwillingness to compromise his views.

The Role of Hubris

After putting $2 million into the software development more than five years ago, the company still has no revenues and no installations and therefore, no referenceable accounts to move the product forward. Eventually, some competitor will solve the problem that this entrepreneur solved many years ago. Once again, an extraordinarily valuable product was prevented from reaching the marketplace because of entrepreneurial hubris.

Chapter 14

What We Can Learn from CEOs when Hubris Is Not an Issue

"Outstanding leaders go out of their way to boost the self-esteem of their personnel. If people believe in themselves, it's amazing what they can accomplish."

- Sam Walton

I have two primary reasons for including Jerre Stead and Howard Matthews in this book. The first is to acknowledge that they are two of the best CEOs with whom I have ever had the privilege of working, and the second reason is to identify the most important five ingredients in their management styles and operating principles that allowed them to be so successful while at the same time attracting, engaging and retaining executive talent and doing so without hubris.

1. Both executives were rigorous about getting their staffs together on a weekly basis. In both cases, "staff" meant all direct reports and, in some cases, executives who had responsibility for highly visible or special projects. In Jerre's case, it meant a 2 ½ hour meeting that typically occurred on Tuesdays at both Ingram Micro and IHS. In Howard's case, as a former retail executive, it was a 2-hour staff meeting on Mondays. It should be noted that although some of the entrepreneurs described in this book conducted staff meetings, none did so on a

regular basis. The agendas for these meetings with both Jerre and Howard were strikingly similar. Early in the meeting there was an opportunity for the CEO to bring to his staff the most important issues that needed to be addressed followed by an open discussion. An open discussion of what might be called "old business" then followed. Topics included significant customer opportunities and challenges, bonus pools and allocations, HR policies and practices, financial reporting including projections, budgets and run rates. Both CEOs concluded meetings with a roundtable where attendees could identify their top three priorities with strong encouragement to identify support from others in the room that would contribute to success.

2. Another similarity between the management styles of these two great CEOs is their intense focus on what were the highest priorities. The following anecdote describes Jerre's intense focus which I observed during one of the first staff meetings that I attended under Jerre's leadership at Ingram Micro.

Jerre was new to the company and was building a new executive staff. At one of the first meetings, he asked each of us to be prepared to discuss our top three priorities at the following week's meeting. I came in with seven, the person next to me with nine and one of the other executives had 17. After we began to discuss our priorities and he realized that none of us had honored his request to identify the top three he asked us "what part of three do you not understand?" He then suggested that we focus on the top three most important tasks and pointed out that as soon as one was successfully completed we could then add a new one to the top three. He then strongly suggested that rather than spend the rest of the staff meeting on the objectives we had brought in, the time would be better utilized by our returning to our desks and clearly identifying the top three for the staff meeting the following week.

The other entrepreneurs in this book had great difficulty clearly identifying what were the most important drivers to the business success in the short, intermediate and long-term.

3. Third, both Howard and Jerre were very approachable and in constant communication with employees as well as their staff. Tom Peters, in his book, *Management by Walking Around*, addresses the importance of this notion with the observation that employees pay great attention to how the CEO and executive leadership is spending its time. To call this an open-door policy is not adequate because the way that phrase is generally used does not encapsulate the open flow of information and the employee engagement that both executives were able to secure.

4. The fourth similarity is in the way each of these CEOs encouraged both staff and executives to strive for excellence in their performance. The quote used above to introduce the chapter on Jerre Stead, "every morning I wake up committed to helping great people do great things" reflects the way both executives operated.

5. The fifth and final similarity is how they dealt with mistakes and errors. They were very clear that executives were always accountable

for decisions and execution. The best example I know relates to an incident with Howard. Midway through the third quarter, my organization presented numbers to the CFO related to software licensing expenses. The numbers we presented were significantly below the actuals that came through and adversely affected forecasts that we gave to the board about quarterly performance only a few weeks earlier. It became clear to me that had I done additional homework on this important issue, I could have avoided putting Howard in an embarrassing position with the board. Because of Howard's openness and style, I took it to him immediately upon discovery. I openly admitted that I had not taken adequate steps to ensure that the forecast we presented was materially accurate. I must say that the way he operated meant that the bad news was quickly revealed, acknowledged and a course of remedial steps were quickly deployed.

I'm sure that there are many successful companies that have CEOs who do not rigorously apply these five ingredients to their operations. In fact, deploying these five is in no way a guarantee that the company will be successful. However, what I think we can learn from these two superior CEOs is that the probability of success goes up significantly when they are in place.

Chapter 15

What We Can Learn from Entrepreneurs Who Kill Their Companies

"If you are standing upright, do not fear a crooked shadow."

- Chinese Proverb

There are at least four themes in the above stories that are worthy of further review and evaluation.

1. ***"I know what's best, so the law doesn't matter."***

There are four chapters above that describe situations where the entrepreneur broke the law. In Chapters 1, 4 and 5, the violations were detected and the results were fines or imprisonment. In Chapter 4, of course, Henry, who was convicted, is still a fugitive from justice. In Chapter 12, the entrepreneurs have engaged in activities that are very likely to have been illegal, but a final determination has not been made. The lessons to be learned from the above chapters include the danger that there are entrepreneurs who believe that the law does not apply to them. In Chapter 1, Peter, was eventually brought down by the IRS. In Chapter 4, Henry was eventually brought down by the

FBI, the Department of Justice and the Securities and Exchange Commission. In Chapter 5, Paul pleaded guilty to eight counts of felony fraud for embezzling more than $8 million from an escrow company he ran. Chapter 12 describes potentially fraudulent misrepresent-tations within the accounting system and are likely to be the subject of penalties by the IRS.

2. ***"Minority interests do not matter ... at all ... (except in the beginning, of course)"***

In five chapters above, Chapters 3, 6, 10, 11 and 12, entrepreneurs demonstrated total disregard for minority interests. To my knowledge none have paid a penalty for this lack of concern for small and often early and instrumental investors.

In one case related to Chapter 6, minority shareholders pledged their shares against a large potential lawsuit settlement with only the entrepreneur's assertion about the value of the shares that were pledged. The entrepreneur never took decisive action to clarify how much trouble the shareholders were in when adverse decisions by their company meant that they would have to clearly identify the value of the shares that they had pledged and were substantially "under water." Unfortunately, employees, who held options on shares and therefore had potential rights as shareholders, were often not considered in any actions of the company.

In the case of Chapter 12, an officer was promised at least 2% of the company in his offer letter and nine months later had not received any clarification as to how many shares that meant or any arrangement under which he would be granted those shares under a vesting schedule.

Chapter 10 also describes the situation where in conversations over a period of the year, the entrepreneur never raised the issue of how early investors and minority shareholders would be treated.

3. ***"Don't question me, I have super powers in negotiation, among many others."***

As described in Chapter 2, Michael negotiated what he described as "the most incredible discounts in the history of computer purchasing." His commitment to purchase 10,000 machines over a few years without any definitive plan for developing the software for those machines created a situation where the unearned discount was so substantial that the company's headquarters building (reaching the final stages of construction) was turned over to the computer company as partial payment for the unearned discount.

In Chapter 11, Chuck believed he was the only one that could meet with customers and potential customers. Having listened to him on more than a few occasions and watched him interact with customers, it became clear that one of the reasons he felt so strongly that only he could negotiate was his ability to fabricate evidence of his earlier successes.

In Chapter 12, Craig routinely and openly criticized executives that reported to him for the results of their negotiations and believed that the result of his lack of involvement cost the company hundreds of thousands of dollars over a period of a few months.

4. ***"I have a great product for a particular market, but it can do so much more."***

In Chapter 2, Michael demonstrated that although the technology which led to the creation of a new and disruptive technology for cash register and retail automation systems, was not suited for the hospitality industry. There were certain limitations in the technology that simply could not be overcome for some of the fundamental requirements for this market. In Chapter 13, the entrepreneur continued to argue for the expansion of the applicability of the software in which he had invested millions of his own money. And so there were no sales into a marketplace that had a potential of $50 billion. There were also no sales into any of the other legacy marketplaces.

Summary

I suspect that a more exhaustive review and analysis of entrepreneurial hubris will bring other lessons. I only hope that this book meets the objectives as laid out in the Foreword and stimulates further analysis so that both investors and entrepreneurs can be significantly more successful.

Appendix A
Quotes and Sources for Chapter 4

Brief Timeline Overview

1986: Gemstar founded in Pasadena, California

1999-2000: Period during which merger talks between Gemstar and TV Guide occur. Eventually the Department of Justice determined illegal collusion and levied the largest find of its type in U.S. history: $5.67 million).

1999-2002: Period of suspected accounting irregularities

2000: Department of Justice (DoJ) approves merger of Gemstar and TV Guide

2002-April: Gemstar-TV Guide loses $3 billion in market cap after accounting irregularities are announced.

2002-October: SEC begins investigation of accountting practices during 1999-2002

2002-October: Henry resigns from role as CEO

2003-February: DoJ announces agreement to settle pre-merger illegal coordination between Gemstar and TV Guide: fine of $5.67 million

2003-June: SEC alleges $248 million overstatement of revenues for Gemstar-TV Guide

2005-May: Court decision to escrow $29.5 million for Henry (and $8.2 million for Elsie) rather than pay it out

2005-September: SEC announces Henry will plead guilty to obstruction of justice in SEC probe

2006-January: SEC criticizes DoJ Plea Bargain with Henry Yuen

2006-March: Henry convicted of securities fraud

2008-April: 9th District Court affirms ruling of securities fraud against Henry

2008-April: SEC stops severance for Henry of $29.5 million

2008-May: SEC indictment - Henry accused of deleting e-mails after subpoena was issued

2008-May: Obstruction charges against Henry – "US v. Henry C. Yuen"

2008-May: Henry declared "fugitive from justice" by DoJ

Chapter 4 References

A1

2000-July: Gemstar-TV Guide merger gets DoJ OK

"TV Guide and Gemstar were given the go-ahead to merge last week by the Department of Justice, creating an electronic-programming-guide (EPG) behemoth, given TV Guide's brand recognition, Gemstar's reach and, more important, Gemstar's patents. The new company will be called Gemstar-TV Guide International, and Henry Yuen will serve as chairman and CEO.

"The approval ends a process that began last October when Gemstar announced it would buy TV Guide. The $9.2 billion stock-and-debt deal gave Gemstar shareholders 55% of the combined company. And the fears from competitors are that the two companies, which are No. 1 and 2 in their market, will dominate EPG services.

"Another issue facing the EPG market is Gemstar's patents, which some believe can slow competitive growth. Boylan says the company is still in litigation with Scientific-Atlanta, Pioneer, General Instruments/Motorola and TiVo. 'We'd like to negotiate a reasonable settlement with any of those parties,' adds Boylan. 'We don't like to litigate, but if someone chooses to flagrantly disregard our intellectual property, we have no choice but to protect it. And when companies like Microsoft, AOL and Sony legitimately license the technology, we have to protect their investments as well.'

"Gary Lieberman, broadband technology/interactive television analyst for Morgan Stanley Dean Witter, says the outcome of those lawsuits will have a great impact on the position the new company holds in the market. 'If Gemstar is found to have a lot of the ones that they claim, then TV Guide and Gemstar will be in a powerful position,' he adds."

SOURCE: Massive new company could dominate EPG market: By Ken Kerschbaumer

A2

2003-February: JUSTICE DEPARTMENT REACHES SETTLEMENT WITH GEMSTAR-TV GUIDE FOR ILLEGAL PRE-MERGER COORDINATION: Department Obtains Record Civil Penalties of $5.67 Million and Injunction

"The Department of Justice today announced a settlement with Gemstar-TV Guide International Inc. that requires the company to pay a record $5.67 million in civil penalties and agree to certain restrictions to resolve the Department's allegations that Gemstar and TV Guide had fixed prices, allocated customers, and violated pre-merger waiting period requirements prior to their merger in July 2000. The civil penalties are the highest ever paid in a case of this type known as 'gun jumping.'

"The Department today filed a civil antitrust complaint in U.S. District Court for the District of Columbia along with a proposed consent decree that, if approved by the Court, would resolve the lawsuit.

"The Department's complaint alleges that, starting in mid-1999, Gemstar and TV Guide agreed to stop competing for customers, decided together on prices and terms to be offered, and jointly managed their interactive program guide business during the mandatory pre-merger waiting period of the Hart-Scott-Rodino (HSR) Act of 1976. Under the Act, the parties are required to keep their operations separate so that the Department of Justice can review the merger. The Department said that their 'gun jumping' conduct violated the HSR Act, as well as

Section 1 of the Sherman Antitrust Act

"Merging parties must remain separate and independent until the end of the statutory waiting period," said R. Hewitt Pate, Acting Assistant Attorney General in charge of the Department's Antitrust Division. “A plan to merge in the future does not justify price fixing, customer allocation, or otherwise combining their businesses, while the Justice Department is investigating the competitive effects of the transaction.”

“The proposed consent decree prevents Gemstar-TV Guide from engaging in similar conduct in the future and gives customers that signed contracts with TV Guide during the pre-merger period a chance to rescind those contracts.

“Prior to mid-1999, Gemstar and TV Guide competed to provide interactive program guides, or IPGs, to cable and satellite television service providers. IPGs allow television viewers to use the television remote to view program schedule information and select programs for viewing.

“The complaint alleged that Gemstar and TV Guide stopped competing for some customers in June 1999, while they were negotiating a possible joint venture between their two companies. They subsequently announced that they would merge in October 1999 and filed a pre-merger notification under the HSR Act. Pending consummation of the transaction, and while the Department of Justice conducted its review of the transaction, Gemstar and TV Guide secretly agreed to allocate markets and customers between them, agreed on the prices and material terms that customers would be offered, and began jointly conducting their IPG business. The complaint alleged that this conduct lessened competition between TV Guide and Gemstar in violation of Section 1 of the Sherman Act, and gave Gemstar premature control over TV Guide in violation of the HSR Act.

"The HSR Act requires companies planning acquisitions or mergers that meet certain thresholds to file pre-merger notification documents with the Justice Department and the Federal Trade Commission. The HSR Act also requires that the merging parties observe a mandatory waiting period, after which the companies may go ahead with the transaction. The purpose of the waiting period is to give the antitrust agencies an opportunity to investigate proposed transactions, and determine whether they would violate the antitrust laws, so that if the government determines that a transaction violates the antitrust laws, it may seek to block that transaction before the waiting period expires. Parties are subject to a maximum civil penalty of $11,000 per day for each day they have been found to be in violation of the HSR Act.

"The proposed Final Judgment, filed along with the complaint, seeks a total civil penalty of $5.67 million, reflecting the maximum civil penalties of $11,000 per day per company.

"Gemstar-TV Guide, a Delaware corporation with its principal place of business in Pasadena, California, was formed when Gemstar merged with TV Guide in July 2000. It had annual revenues of about $1.4 billion for the year ending December 31, 2001, and revenues for the fiscal year ending March 31, 2000, of about $241 million.

"TV Guide Inc., now a wholly-owned subsidiary of Gemstar-TV Guide International Inc., is a Delaware corporation with its principal place of business in Tulsa, Oklahoma. For the fiscal year ending December 31, 1999, TV Guide reported revenue of about $1.1 billion.

"As required by the Tunney Act, the proposed consent decree will be published in the Federal Register, along with the Department's competitive impact statement. Any person may submit comments concerning the proposed decree during a

60-day waiting period to James R. Wade, Chief, Litigation III, Antitrust Division, U.S. Department of Justice, 325 7th Street, N.W., Washington, D.C. 20530. After the 60-day comments period, the court may enter the consent decree upon finding that it serves the public interest.

SOURCE: THURSDAY, FEBRUARY 6, 2003 (202) 514-2007 WWW.USDOJ.GOV

A3

2005-September: Ex-Gemstar Chairman to Plead Guilty

"Henry C. Yuen, former chairman of Gemstar-TV Guide International Inc., will plead guilty to obstructing a Securities and Exchange Commission investigation into alleged accounting irregularities at the company from 1999 to 2002", the U.S. attorney's office said Tuesday.

"Under terms of a plea agreement with prosecutors, the 57-year-old Yuen will serve six months of home detention during a two-year period of probation.

"He also will be required to contribute $1 million to charities representing low-income victims of fraud and to pay a $250,000 fine, the prosecutor's office said.

"Yuen and the Los Angeles-based company's chief financial officer, Elsie Leung, were forced out in late 2002 after Gemstar was discovered to have inflated revenue by nearly $250 million.

SOURCE: September 21, 2005 | David Rosenzweig | Times Staff Writer

A4

2006-January: SEC Chastises Ex-Gemstar Exec Plea Bargain

"The U.S. Securities and Exchange Commission has openly criticized the Justice Department's plea agreement with former Gemstar CEO Henry Yuen, telling a judge that prosecutors may have been too lenient in settling with the embattled executive.

In response, Judge John Walter has delayed the approval of the plea deal, which mandated six months of home detention and a $1 million charitable donation.

SOURCE: Marius Meland, Law360

A5

2006-March: Ex-Gemstar Chief Liable in Fraud

"A federal judge found the former chief executive of Gemstar–TV Guide Henry C Yuen liable for securities fraud, according to a ruling unsealed on Monday in a federal regulatory lawsuit that claimed Mr. Yuen inflated the company's revenue by $248 million to increase its stock.

"Federal District Judge Mariana R. Pfaelzer also found Mr. Yuen liable for misrepresenting facts to Gemstar's auditor and falsifying its books."

SOURCE: The Associated Press. March 21, 2006

A6

2006-May: Former Chairman and CEO of Gemstar-TV Guide International, Inc. Ordered to Pay Over $22 Million for Role in Accounting Fraud

"The Securities and Exchange Commission today announced that Henry C. Yuen, the former chairman and chief executive officer of Gemstar-TV Guide International, Inc., has been ordered to pay over $22 million for his role in a scheme to defraud investors by inflating Gemstar's licensing and advertising revenues. In addition, Yuen will be permanently barred from serving as an officer or director of a public company.

"After a three-week trial in December 2005, in the Central District of California, United States District Judge Mariana R. Pfaelzer found in favor of the Commission and against Yuen on all of the SEC's charges. The court found that Yuen had committed securities fraud by making misrepresentations and omissions of material fact about certain Gemstar revenues, that Yuen aided and abetted Gemstar's primary violations of the periodic reporting and record keeping control requirements, and that Yuen lied to Gemstar's auditors.

"On May 8, 2006, the court ordered Yuen to pay a total of $22,327,231 in disgorgement, penalties, and interest, and entered a permanent injunction against future securities law violations and a permanent bar from serving as an officer or director of a public company. The court found that Yuen received $10,577,692 in ill-gotten gains from his fraudulent conduct, consisting of (1) $3,022,452 in gross bonus compensation received by Yuen during the period of the fraud, and (2) $7,555,240 in excess trading profit he received by selling Gemstar stock during the period of the fraud. The court ordered Yuen to pay a civil money penalty equal to the amount of disgorgement.

"'We are pleased that the district court so soundly rejected Henry Yuen's attempts to evade responsibility for the fraud he orchestrated at Gemstar-TV Guide,' said Randall R. Lee, the SEC's Pacific regional director. 'The final judgment and the permanent bar against future service as an officer or director reflect the seriousness of Yuen's misconduct and the vital importance of punishing and deterring securities law violations which harm the investing public.'

"Gemstar is a Los Angeles-based media and technology company that publishes TV Guide magazine and an interactive program guide (IPG) for televisions that enables consumers to navigate through and select television programs. During the relevant period, Gemstar generated revenues from the IPG by licensing the technology to third parties and selling advertising on the IPG. In statements to securities analysts and the investing public, Gemstar repeatedly touted the IPG technology and IPG advertising revenues as the company's future and as the 'value driver' of the company's stock, and downplayed expected declines in revenue from TV Guide magazine. When Gemstar announced for the first time that certain of its IPG licensing and advertising revenue may have been improperly recorded, its stock price declined by approximately 37%, causing a market loss in excess of $3 billion.

"The SEC's complaint, filed in June 2003, alleges that from June 1999 through September 2002, Gemstar overstated its total revenues by at least $248 million to meet its ambitious projections for revenue growth from IPG licensing and advertising. The complaint further alleges that Yuen directed and approved Gemstar's fraudulent recording of IPG licensing and advertising revenue and approved fraudulent disclosure documents. The complaint alleges that Yuen knew, but did not disclose, that

Gemstar was improperly recognizing and reporting licensing and advertising revenue from seven companies and that he participated in fraudulently diverting revenue from one business sector to another to meet sector revenue projections. Additionally, the complaint alleges that Yuen signed false management representation letters to Gemstar's auditors regarding the structure of certain transactions.

"The complaint charges Yuen with securities fraud, falsifying Gemstar's books and records, aiding and abetting Gemstar's reporting and record-keeping violations, and making false statements to auditors, in violation of Section 17(a) of the Securities Act of 1933 and Sections 10(b), 13(a), 13(b)(2)(A), 13(b)(2)(B) and 13(b)(5) of the Securities Exchange Act of 1934 and Rules 10b-5, 12b-20, 13a-1, 13a-11, 13a-13, 13b2-1, and 13b2-2 thereunder.

SOURCE: U.S. SECURITIES AND EXCHANGE COMMISSION, Litigation Release No. 19694 / May 10, 2006, SEC v. Henry C. Yuen, Civil Action No. CV 03-4376 MRP (PLAx) (C.D. Cal.)

A7

2008-May: Feds Indict Ex-Gemstar Chief

"Former Gemstar-TV Guide International chairman Henry Yuen was indicted Tuesday on a felony charge that he obstructed a Securities and Exchange Commission investigation into Gemstar's alleged accounting irregularities.

"In October 2002, the SEC began a formal investigation of Gemstar and its accounting activities from 1999-2002. Yuen was among those subpoenaed in the investigation, which required him to provide to investigators several items including all handwritten, typed or electronic correspondence and other documents concerning Gemstar.

"The subpoena included documents on Yuen's computer. But according to the indictment, after Yuen received his subpoena, he deleted e-mails and Gemstar corporate documents.

"Whether Yuen will ever answer to the charges is a mystery. He has disappeared, and the federal government is asking anybody who knows of his whereabouts to contact the FBI in Los Angeles."

SOURCE: 5:00 AM PDT 5/14/2008 by Leslie Simmons, Associated Press

A8

2008-May: Former Gemstar CEO Yuen Hit With Obstruction Charge

"Henry C. Yuen, the former chairman and chief executive of Gemstar-TV Guide International Inc., was charged by the Justice Department with obstructing an investigation into accounting irregularities.

"Yuen was charged with a felony count of obstructing a Securities and Exchange Commission probe of alleged irregularities at Gemstar from 1999 through 2002, the department said in a statement Tuesday.

"The Justice Department said Yuen deleted from his computer documents that the SEC had sought in its investigation. It also said that the day before he was supposed to testify before the agency in 2003, he manipulated his computer to make it impossible to recover the deleted documents.

"David Scheper, a lawyer for Yuen, and Carolyn Newburn, a spokeswoman for Gemstar's parent company, Macrovision Solutions Corp. in Santa Clara, Calif., didn't return calls seeking comment.

"In an SEC civil lawsuit two years ago, a federal judge in Los Angeles found Yuen liable for securities fraud for misleading investors and auditors by inflating sales from 1999 to 2002. Yuen was ordered to pay $22.3 million in fines and forfeitures.

"In a hearing last year, an SEC lawyer said Yuen has made no effort to pay the judgment and had about $150 million in assets outside the U.S.

"Gemstar-TV Guide, whose technology helps pay-TV customers navigate the 500-channel universe with an on-screen program guide, was bought May 2 by Macrovision in a deal initially valued at $2.8 billion in cash and stock."

SOURCE: May 14, 2008 | From Los Angeles Times Staff and Wire Reports

A9

2008-May: Former Chairman and CEO Of Gemstar-TV Guide International, Inc. Charged With Obstruction of an SEC Investigation

"The Securities and Exchange Commission announced that on May 13, 2008, Henry C. Yuen, the former chairman and chief executive officer of Gemstar-TV Guide International, Inc., was indicted on a felony charge of obstructing a Commission investigation.

"The indictment alleges that during an investigation regarding accounting irregularities at Gemstar-TV Guide, the Commission issued a subpoena to Yuen requiring him to produce documents. After receiving the subpoena, Yuen allegedly began deleting from his computer various documents that were called for by the subpoena. In addition, the day before Yuen was scheduled to appear for testimony in the Commission investigation, Yuen allegedly ran a program on his computer that made it impossible to recover the documents he had previously deleted.

"The SEC's complaint, filed in June 2003, alleged that from June 1999 through September 2002, Yuen participated in Gemstar's fraudulent overstatement of revenues by at least $248 million to meet its ambitious financial projections. After a three-week trial in December 2005, the court found in favor of the Commission and against Yuen on all claims including securities fraud and ordered Yuen, among other things, to pay over $22 million in disgorgement and penalties. On April 1, 2008, the Ninth Circuit affirmed the district court's ruling finding that Yuen committed securities fraud, and found the court ordered disgorgement and penalty against Yuen was appropriate."

SOURCE: U.S. SECURITIES AND EXCHANGE COMMISSION, Litigation Release No. 20599 / May 23, 2008, U.S. v. Henry C. Yuen, No. CR 08-00567 (C.D. Cal.)

A10

2008-May: Gemstar-TV Guide Ex-CEO Now Wanted For Obstruction

"Federal authorities said Thursday that former Gemstar-TV Guide International Inc. chairman Henry Yuen is a fugitive after he was indicted on a felony obstruction charge that carries a possible five-year prison term.

"Yuen was convicted in federal court in 2006 of securities fraud for inflating Gemstar's revenue by $248 million to boost its stock price.

"Gemstar and its TV Guide channel listing service were acquired this month by Macrovision Solutions Corp. for $2.3 billion in cash and stock.

"The indictment against Yuen, filed Tuesday in U.S. District Court in Los Angeles, charges him with deleting documents and e-mails from his computer that the Securities and Exchange Commission sought in the earlier prosecution.

"'I'll call him a fugitive,' said U.S. Attorney spokesman Thom Mrozek. 'We don't know where he is right now. And by now, he should be aware of the charges against him.'

"The U.S. Attorney directed those with information about Yuen's whereabouts to contact the FBI.

"Yuen's lawyer, David Scheper, did not immediately return a message seeking comment.

"'Yuen has failed to pay the $22.3 million in fines and penalties from his conviction in the Securities and Exchange Commission case.' That judgment was affirmed by the 9th U.S. Circuit Court of Appeals in April.

"The court said the later revelation of the fraud caused the company to lose $3 billion in market value after it corrected its accounts.

"The SEC has been unable to seize Yuen's assets and claimed in a previous court filing that he gave $42 million to third parties and moved substantial amounts of cash offshore in an attempt to evade seizures of his assets.

"SEC senior trial counsel John Bulgozdy said he expected Yuen to pay eventually.

"'We fully expect that now that the 9th Circuit has ruled that Mr. Yuen will honor the judgment,' Bulgozdy said.

"A spokesman for Santa Clara, Calif. based Macro-vision Solutions Corp. declined to comment on the matter."

SOURCE: Associated Press, May 15, 2008

A11

2008-May: Ex-Gemstar-TV Guide CEO Yuen Now Fugitive

"Henry Yuen, the former CEO of Gemstar-TV Guide International, is now considered a fugitive from justice by the U.S. government for failing to turn himself in to authorities after being charged with obstruction of justice by the U.S. Attorney in Los Angeles.

"Yuen had been convicted in 2006 of securities fraud for lying about Gemstar-TV Guide's revenues to inflate the stock price. The new obstruction of justice charge alleges he destroyed documents and emails sought by the Securities and Exchange Commission in relation to this earlier investigation.

"The ex-CEO's apparent flight from justice and failure to pay $22.3 million in fines for securities fraud, lying to auditors and falsifying Gemstar's books to inflate the company's revenues by $248 million in 2000-2002, comes as an unwelcome reminder of the woes that have afflicted Gemstar-TV Guide, which was acquired by Macrovision on May 2 for $2.3 billion.

"As the publication struggled to keep pace with the explosion of cable TV options, then the emergence of online video, TV Guide's ad pages fell 65%, from 3,195 in 2000 to just 926 in 2006--recovering slightly to 1,138 in 2007 after the title's relaunch as a full-sized magazine.

"Market capitalization of the company, which also has a substantial electronic guide business, fell from $20 billion in 2000 to just $2 billion in 2007. After Yuen's fraud was revealed in April 2002, the company lost about $3 billion in market value.

"After Yuen's ouster in October 2002 at the behest of shareholder News Corp., Gemstar-TV Guide moved aggressively to break with the past and diversify its business, probably with an eye toward the eventual sale of the company. CEO Jeff Shell, who steered the company through the worst of the post-Yuen PR storm, patched up relations with News Corp. before handing the reins over to CEO Richard Battista in December 2004.

"Around the time of Yuen's conviction in May 2006, Battista appointed a new executive vice president of product management, Steve Shannon, in January 2006, a new executive vice president of sales and services, Tom Carson, in April 2006, and a new general counsel, Stephen Yu, as well as a new executive vice president of corporate marketing, Corey Ferengul, both in May 2006."

SOURCE: Media Daily News by Erik Sass @eriksass1, May 19, 2008

Appendix B

United States Court of Appeals, Ninth Circuit. SECURITIES AND EXCHANGE COMMISSION, Plaintiff-Appellee, Henry C. Yuen; Elsie M. Leung, Intervenors-Appellants, v. GEMSTAR-TV GUIDE INTERNATIONAL, INC., Defendant.

(Selected sections)

No. 03-56129.
Decided: May 12, 2004

FACTS

On August 14, 2002, Gemstar, a Delaware corporation, announced that it was auditing the operations of its Technology and Licensing Sector and Interactive Platform Sector after finding that 2001 revenues and related amortization for these sectors had been overstated by some $40 million. On November 7, 2002, Gemstar announced plans to restructure its management and corporate governance.

As part of the restructuring plans, Gemstar entered into negotiations for termination agreements with its Chief Executive Officer ("CEO"), Dr. Henry Yuen, and its Chief Operating Officer ("COO") and Chief Financial Officer ("CFO"), Elsie Ma Leung. Dr. Yuen's termination agreement provided for a "termination fee" of $22,452,640, an additional $7,030,778 in unpaid salary, bonuses, and unused vacation time, and 5,274,519 shares of restricted stock. Ms. Leung was to receive a termination fee of $6,957,953, an additional $1,209,695 in unpaid salary, bonuses, and unused vacation time, 1,126,504 shares of common stock, and 353,680 shares of restricted stock. Additionally, Yuen agreed to serve as the non-executive chairman of the board and Leung agreed to a position as an employee in the international business department. The arrangements for Yuen's and Leung's compensation are collectively referred to as the Restructuring Payments.

On October 15, 2002, before the Yuen and Leung termination agreements were in final form, attorneys for the Securities and Exchange Commission ("SEC") met with counsel for Gemstar, Yuen, and Leung, and requested that the Restructuring Payments be placed in escrow. On October 17, 2002, the SEC ordered a formal investigation into the announced overvaluation of the revenue and profits from some of Gemstar's sectors. On October 23, 2002, Yuen and Leung notified the SEC that they declined to submit to a voluntary escrow.

On October 28, 2002, as part of its investigation, the SEC issued testimonial subpoenas to Gemstar's Board of Directors. Yuen and Leung contend that in response to the subpoenas Gemstar sent a draft escrow agreement for the Restructuring Payments to the SEC on November 6, 2002. Hours before the restructuring agreements were to be executed on November 7, 2002, Gemstar informed Yuen and Leung's attorney that the Restructuring Payments were to be placed in escrow for six months, and that such escrow provision was non-negotiable. Yuen and Leung acceded to the six-month escrow in "side letters" executed that day.

On March 31, 2003, Appellants Yuen and Leung filed a complaint in district court against the SEC, objecting to the escrow, seeking injunctive and declaratory relief, and requesting a temporary restraining order to unblock and dissolve the escrow to allow the restructuring payments to be made. According to a declaration by Appellants' counsel, "Gemstar is contractually obligated to release the Restructuring Payments to Plaintiffs on May 6, 2003." Appellants' counsel also maintained that the escrow impermissibly interfered with Yuen's and Leung's property rights to receive the Restructuring Payments, and that the escrowed payments did not constitute "extraordinary payments" under section 1103 of Sarbanes-Oxley. Following an April 21, 2003 hearing, the district court denied Appellants' request for a preliminary injunction, finding that the side letters constituted consent by Yuen and Leung to the initial escrow, set to expire May 6, 2003. The district court did not address whether the restructuring payments qualified as "extraordinary payments" under section 1103.

On May 5, 2003, the SEC filed an application with the district court to place the Restructuring Payments in a 45-day escrow account pursuant to Section 1103. In a declaration filed with the application, an attorney for the SEC described the ongoing investigation of Gemstar. The district court sua sponte ordered the parties to maintain the status quo and requested additional briefing. A hearing was held on May 9, 2003. On May 12, 2003, the district court entered an order granting the SEC's application to place the Restructuring Payments in escrow and directed the parties to prepare a joint order to affect such escrow. Appellants filed a motion to reconsider the escrow order on May 22, 2003. After a status conference on May 29, 2003, the court denied Appellants' motion to reconsider and entered the joint order of escrow. The order specifically described the disputed funds as "extraordinary payments" subject to section 1103 and directed that they be held in interest-bearing accounts for 45 days.

On June 19, 2003, the SEC commenced a civil action in the Central District of California, No. 03-CV-4376, alleging Yuen and Leung had fraudulently inflated Gemstar's revenue reports by $223 million, in violation of various sections of the Securities Acts of 1933 and 1934. The SEC also filed an application to have the escrow continued indefinitely for the duration of the action against Yuen and Leung.

On June 20, 2003, on the government's ex parte motion, the district court extended the temporary escrow for an additional 45 days. The district court reiterated its finding that the payments were "extraordinary payments" within the meaning of section 1103 and rejected Appellants' contentions that the statute was unconstitutionally vague. On June 24, 2003, the district court entered an order directing the maintenance of the escrow for the duration of the SEC's civil action.

Yuen and Leung filed a notice of interlocutory appeal on July 2, 2003. Appellants contend section 1103(1) is void for vagueness; (2) effects an unreasonable seizure of their property in violation of the Fourth Amendment; (3) does not retroactively apply to the payments in this case that had already been contracted to be paid or had already been made prior to the enactment of the statute; and (4) does not apply to the disputed payments, which are not “extraordinary payments” for the purposes of Sarbanes-Oxley.

III

SECTION 1103

Section 1103 of the Sarbanes-Oxley Act gives the SEC authority to ensure that assets of an issuer of securities which have been fraudulently obtained are not dissipated during the investigation and litigation of securities fraud cases. See 15 U.S.C. § 78u-3 (2002). Specifically, section 1103 provides that:

[w]henever, during the course of a lawful investigation involving possible violations of the Federal securities laws by an issuer of publicly traded securities or any of its directors, officers, partners, controlling persons, agents, or employees, it shall appear to the Commission that it is likely that the issuer will make extraordinary payments (whether compensation or otherwise) to any of the foregoing persons, the Commission may petition a Federal district court for a temporary order requiring the issuer to escrow, subject to court supervision, those payments in an interest-bearing account for 45 days.

Section 1103 authorizes one additional 45-day extension of the temporary escrow order on a showing of good cause. 15 U.S.C. § 78u-3(c)(3)(A)(iv). However, once the subject of an investigation is charged with a securities violation by the commencement of a civil action, "the order shall remain in effect, subject to court approval, until the conclusion of any legal proceedings related thereto, and the affected issuer or other person, shall have the right to petition the court for review of the order." 15 U.S.C. § 78u-3(c)(3)(B)(i).

Sarbanes-Oxley does not define "extraordinary payments." The SEC is empowered to adopt regulations for the implementation of Sarbanes-Oxley. See 15 U.S.C. § 78w. To date the SEC has not done so. Neither Congress nor the SEC has given any indication as to the meaning of the words "extraordinary payments."

IV

2. Statutory Construction

This appeal presents issues of statutory construction of the term "extraordinary payments." In its June 20, 2003 order, the district court correctly noted, "'extraordinary' in common parlance essentially means 'out of the ordinary' or 'unusual.' Unusual, of course, is a comparative adjective that has meaning only in relation to what is 'usual.' " District Court's June 20, 2003 Memorandum of Decision at 9 (emphasis added). This observation has value only if properly applied. Unfortunately, it was not.

"... ordinarily, one could determine what was 'extraordinary' and 'abnormal,' or not normal, only by comparison with what was established to be normal." Bjelland & Co., Inc. v. United States, 45 Cust. Ct. 435, 442 (Cust.Ct., Jul. 26, 1960) (on appeal for reappraisement of imported goods, affirming customs appraiser's valuation of good exchanged in the "ordinary course of trade"). Here, plaintiff SEC limited its proof in its section 1103 application to an investigating attorney's affidavit (Cebeci Declaration, Excerpts of Record at 111-58). The affidavit incontestably established the first element of section 1103: that an SEC investigation was under way. 15 U.S.C. § 78u-3(c)(3)(B)(i).

However, the affidavit-and consequently the record-is completely silent regarding what constituted usual or ordinary payments upon termination of a CEO and Chairman of the Board (Yuen) or COO and CFO (Leung) under the same or similar circumstances to those existing at the time that Appellants ended their employment with Gemstar. Absent any such proof, the district court erroneously substituted two conclusory statements of what was "extraordinary" without concomitant proof of what was "ordinary," and an SEC filing, required under a standard different from that of section 1103.

First, the district court found that the negotiation of the termination agreements for Appellants was "extraordinary" because of the various groups that participated in the negotiations and because the negotiations occurred over a five-month period. Members of the Board of Directors, officers of the corporation, and compensation consultants, accountants, and attorneys for both sides negotiated the restructuring agreements. Nothing in the record suggests this extended negotiation constitutes a deviation from the norm for corporate decision-making of this type. While common experience of the district court might help to determine what is the usual way to negotiate the termination of a lawyer at a law firm or a staff member of the court, common experiences of this kind do not aid judgment in the circumstances of Appellants' termination at Gemstar.

As the declaration of Appellants' counsel shows, Gemstar-TV Guide was the product of a merger between an off-shore company founded by Appellants and TV Guide, a subsidiary of News Corporation, a large telecommunications company. The corporation's earnings before interest, taxes, depreciation and amortization were reported as $242.2 million in the last nine months of 2000. Appellants presented uncontradicted evidence that revenue-producing strategies of Yuen and Leung differed, if not clashed, with those of News Corp. Appellants were interested primarily in raising revenue attributable to the corporation's sales, perhaps not coincidentally to raise their own compensation, which was tied to revenue and profits. The minority owners, Gemstar's current management, were in part interested in publicizing one of their sister corporations through Gemstar's operations, without paying Gemstar any advertising revenue. Such a strategy would increase revenues for the sister corporation, but not for Gemstar. As owners and officers in Gemstar, Appellants would not share in the profits of the sister corporation.

In case Yuen or Leung were terminated "without cause," lengthy and complex employment agreements governed their termination payments. Yuen and Leung had three different components for calculation of their Annual Incentive Bonuses. Complex enough when based on the company's past performance, computations also had to be done for future payments, with the consequent and predictable squabbling over methods for projecting future financial performance.

In view of Gemstar's revenue structure, the conflicting strategies, and the complex schemes for computation of termination payments, it is not surprising that Gemstar would require not only releases, but also representations and warranties from the departing employees. Yet, for all the persons involved in the negotiations, not one presented evidence before the district court that the period or mechanics of the negotiations were out of the ordinary in view of the circumstances. Nor, despite the six-month period between commencement of the investigation (October 17, 2002) and the section 1103 hearing (May 9, 2003), was any expert testimony prepared and presented as to the habits and customs of the marketplace-what was "ordinary"-under the same or similar circumstances.

The second factor on which the district court based its finding that the proposed payments were “extraordinary payments” was their size. We agree that such sums are “extraordinary payments” in relation to what federal judges are paid. However, nothing in section 1103 constrains us to look through such a prism.

There is no evidence in the record of what similarly placed officers and board members of corporations of similar revenues and worth are paid upon termination. Such payments may be called “golden parachutes” or “golden handshakes” in the press, but purple prose is not enough to prove a statutory requirement in court. For enforcement of the securities laws of the United States, evidence of what is “usual” under the same or similar circumstances is necessary to distinguish “extraordinary payments” and to order their impoundment in an escrow pursuant to section 1103.

Last, the district court found it significant that after the termination contracts were finalized, defendant Gemstar chose to report the terms in a Form 8-K filing. A Form 8-K filing is required from an “issuer of securities when substantial events occur .” Scherk v. Alberto-Culver Co., 417 U.S. 506, 528 n. 6, 94 S.Ct. 2449, 41 L.Ed.2d 270 (1974). In this era of heightened corporate vigilance, it is not surprising that Gemstar management should choose to make this report upon the termination of the founders of the company, who were being paid millions of dollars on departure in an amount approximating 15% of the previous year's revenues. But, a discretionary corporate disclosure is not an admission that the company has paid an “extraordinary” amount. In any case, there was also no evidence of whether other “issuers” had made similar reports for similar sums paid to similarly departing upper management under the same or similar circumstances. A “substantial event” may or may not coincide with an “extraordinary payment.” Only evidence of comparable events and circumstances can tell us.

Instead of objective evidence, what we have here is the district court's conjecture as to what would have been "ordinary" or "usual" negotiations for termination payments, conjecture as to what the size should have been of such payments and conclusions drawn from filings made under different standards. The bases used by the district court to judge the negotiations, the payments, and the filing were "irreducibly subjective." cf. Nuñez v. San Diego, 114 F.3d 935, 943 (9th Cir.1997) (considering vagueness challenge to loitering ordinance).

The district court did not need to rely on such subjective bases. Legislation which uses relative adjectives to proscribe activities is not unknown to the law. Statutes and law prohibit "excessive" verdicts (CAL. CIV. PROC. CODE § 657; Fed.R.Civ.P. 59) and sanction "unreasonable" behavior (CAL. CIV. CODE § 1714; Restatement (Second) of Torts, § 281). It is not beyond the judiciary's capacity to interpret and apply statutes which prohibit "excessive" or "unreasonable" amounts. Trial and appellate courts are called upon to do so every day. As to "excessive," see State Farm Ins. Co. v. Campbell, 538 U.S. 408, 123 S.Ct. 1513, 1519-20, 155 L.Ed.2d 585 (2003). But in doing so, the courts are guided by precepts of proportionality and precedent.

Less often, courts are asked whether some remuneration constitutes "extraordinary payment." An example is the line of cases which determines whether payments made by a corporation to an employee is deductible from gross income as an "ordinary and necessary" business expense or is an "extraordinary payment" disallowed as a deduction. See, e.g., LabelGraphics, Inc. v. Commissioner of Internal Revenue, 221 F.3d 1091, 1096 (9th Cir.2000); Elliotts, Inc. v. Commissioner Internal Revenue, 716 F.2d 1241, 1242 (9th Cir.1983).

Whether the adjective is "excessive," "negligent" or "extraordinary," the cases in which those terms appear use similar processes of judgment. The trier-of-fact determines first what constitutes “adequate compensation,” “reasonable care,” or “customary or ordinary payments.” Such determinations require evidence which consists of similar factual situations which can be compared to the case at hand. If the case at hand falls outside the bounds permitted in the comparison cases, that result is deemed “excessive,” “negligent,” or “extraordinary.”

VI

CONCLUSION

For the reasons stated, Appellants' appeal from the June 24, 2003 escrow order is granted, and that order is vacated and remanded for proceedings consistent with this opinion.

The clerk is directed to stay the mandate in this case for 14 calendar days following the filing of this opinion, should the government seek to file a renewed section 1103 request consistent with the standard of proof outlined in this opinion.

VACATED AND REMANDED; the Clerk shall stay the mandate for 14 days after the filing of this opinion.

The principal issue we decide in this case arises in a distinctive statutory context that cannot be ignored or slighted. Judge Wallace cogently explained this important context in SEC v. Rind, 991 F.2d 1486 (9th Cir.1993):

When the [Securities and Exchange] Commission sues to enforce the securities laws, it vindicates public rights and furthers the public interest. The public character of Commission action is reflected in the introduction to the 1934 Act: “[T]ransactions in securities ... are affected with a national public interest which makes it necessary to provide for regulation and control of such transactions.” 15 U.S.C. § 78b. Congress entrusted the Commission with the vital mission of ensuring the honesty and fairness of the capital markets. “The entire purpose and thrust of a [Commission] enforcement action is to expeditiously safeguard the public interest by enjoining securities violations. The claims asserted in such an action stem from, and are colored by, the intense public interest in [Commission] enforcement of these laws." SEC v. Asset Management Corp., 456 F.Supp. 998, 1000 (S.D.Ind.1978).

I

The civil statute under our microscope, Section 1103, 15 U.S.C. § 78u-3(c)(3) is extraordinarily narrow, well defined, and utterly clear. It comes into play only

(1) during the course of a lawful investigation by the Securities and Exchange Commission,

(2) involving possible violations of the federal securities law,

(3) committed by an issuer of publicly traded securities or any of its directors, officers, partners, controlling persons, agents, or employees,

(4) whenever it shall appear to the Commission that it is likely that the issuer will make extraordinary payments to any of those named persons.

II

Faced with one giant corporate scandal after another, Congress' purpose in enacting this mild, temporary measure could not be clearer. One after another, stockholders and others have been left holding an empty bag after corporate insiders engaged in fraud and other corporate crimes at the ultimate expense of the corporation's shareholders and innocent employees. By the time the authorities have been alerted to the fraud, it's too late, the money has already disappeared into the pockets of those who abused their fiduciary responsibilities and the public trust, rendering the traditional remedies used by the Commission to rectify such wrongs-disgorgement, civil penalties, restitution, etc.-difficult if not impossible to pursue. In the meanwhile, the disappearance of such funds impoverishes and damages the issuer itself, once again to the detriment of the shareholders and innocent employees, whose pensions in many cases have been permanently thrashed. Ultimately, our nation is the victim, as the public loses confidence in the stock market.

Section 1103 was initially introduced as Amendment No. 4188, by Senator Trent Lott. See 148 Cong. Rec. S6542 (daily ed. July 10, 2002). In the debate that ensued after Amendment No. 4188's introduction, different senators focused on various possible abuses that Section 1103 was meant to prevent:

Section 3 freezes payments of potential wrongdoers. This section would allow the SEC, during an investigation, to seek an order in Federal court imposing a 45-day freeze on extraordinary payments to corporate executives. Again, this year we have seen just that sort of thing happening. While an investigation is underway, basically rewards were given to those corporate executives. While it would require a court order, there would be this 45-day freeze. The targeted payments would be placed in escrow, ensuring that corporate assets are not improperly taken from [sic] an executive's personal benefit. We have also seen that there are some cases where the law had some loopholes or where it was not timely or where it was not strong enough. One example, of course, is where there has been shredding. Another example is the very bad image of corporate executives taking increased payments, extraordinary payments, while they are being investigated. You can't have that sort of thing.

(Statement of Sen. Lott).

The House of Representatives shared these objectives:

Under this legislation, top executives will not be allowed to pilfer the assets of the company by giving themselves huge bonuses and other extraordinary payments if the company is subject to an [sic] SEC investigation. Their pay and benefits are frozen when the investigation starts. Americans will know that corporate officers will no longer be able to misuse the bankruptcy laws to discharge liabilities based upon securities fraud, and the honest brokers of corporate America will know that those who abuse the law and tarnish corporate America's reputation will go to jail for a long, long time.

148 Cong. Rec. H4685 (daily ed. July 16, 2002) (statement of Rep. Sensenbrenner).

III

The facts and circumstances of this case provide a textbook example of the problem. On April 1, 2002, Gemstar filed its Form 10-K for the year 2001. The filing reported that $107.6 million it had previously claimed as revenue had not actually been realized. Gemstar revealed also that it had previously claimed as substantial revenue receipts from a single "nonmonetary transaction" that was not properly booked. The fall-out from these reevaluations? The next day, Gemstar's stock price declined by a startling 37 percent. But, this was just the beginning. A Form 8-K is a Commission report used to report "material events or corporate changes" that may have an effect on the value of a company's securities. On August 14, 2002, Gemstar announced in a Form 8-K that it intended to restate its 2001 financial results and to reverse $20 million, plus make substantial corrections. Gemstar filed as exhibits to that Form 8-K sworn statements from Yuen and Leung, CEO and CFO respectively, to the effect that they were not able to certify as required by law that some of Gemstar's financial statements were accurate, and that they were not able to comply with Commission orders to do so.

On September 25, 2002, Gemstar filed yet another Form 8-K (1) confirming that it had been notified by NASDAQ that its securities were subject to delisting for failure timely to file a Form 10-Q for the quarter ending on June 30, 2002, (2) that because of an unresolved dispute between Gemstar and its independent auditor KPMG, the company could not file its quarterly Form 10-Q report, and (3) that the resolution of these accounting and financial matters involving restatement of financial statements was "uncertain" and "unpredictable." Clearly, the accounting wheels were falling off this company.

What about Intervenors CEO Yuen and CFO Leung, whose compensation was tied to the performance of Gemstar's reported financial results? On March 27, 2002, all of four days before the revelation to the public about Gemstar's inaccurate revenue claims, Yuen disposed of 7 million Gemstar shares, receiving an initial payment of $59 million. No doubt the purchasers of these shares were duped into believing they were getting fair value for their money, only to see the roof fall in when the facts came publicly to light.

Back at the ranch, and simultaneously with the internal and external unraveling of this creative accounting mess, CEO Yuen and CFO Leung were cutting a new deal with Gemstar's Board to resign from their respective executive positions-but remain as employees-in return for a payment in cash by Gemstar to Yuen of $29.48 million and to Leung of $8.16 million, plus enormous shares of stocks and stock options. Gemstar reported these unusual developments on November 12, 2002, in yet another Form 8-K filing. It is this package of payments around which Yuen and Leung fashion their unconvincing and extraordinary claim that the negotiated payments were not "extraordinary," and that the term "extraordinary" is vague.

Not surprisingly, the Commission finally commenced a formal investigation of this odorific scenario to determine whether Gemstar and its former and present officers and directors had engaged in securities fraud by making materially false and misleading public statements regarding revenue, earnings and losses, etc., for the relevant years.

IV

Here, it is important and instructive to understand what must happen for the Commission to launch an investigation into suspected violations of the securities laws, an action which is a prerequisite to petitioning the court under Section 1103 for a temporary escrow.

Both the Securities Act of 1933 ("Securities Act") and the Securities Exchange Act of 1934 ("Exchange Act") provide the Commission the authority to initiate investigations into suspected violations of the securities laws. See 15 U.S.C. § 77t(a) ("Whenever it shall appear to the Commission ... that the provisions of this subchapter ... have been or are about to be violated, it may ... investigate such facts."); 15 U.S.C. § 78u(a)(1) ("The Commission may ... make such investigations as it deems necessary to determine whether any person has violated, is violating, or is about to violate any provision of this chapter.").

A formal investigation is the process by which the SEC issues subpoenas calling for document production or testimony, supported by the power of the federal courts. To enable the staff of the SEC, rather than the individual, appointed members of the SEC, to perform such an investigation, the Commission must delegate its powers to the staff in a Formal Order of Investigation. That Formal Order of Investigation consists of three parts: 1) a jurisdictional section setting forth the SEC's investigative authority; 2) a probable cause section setting forth the information which, "if true, tends to show" that certain activities have occurred and securities laws have been violated; and 3) a delegation section, containing a statement by the Commission that it is delegating its investigative power to the staff. See Marvin Pickholz, SEC Crimes, § 2:4 (Dec. 2003); see also Am.Jur. Securities, § 1622 (noting that in most circumstances "[n]either a Commission decision whether to conduct a preliminary investigation nor a formal order of investigation is a final order which may be judicially reviewed").

Here, the Formal Order of Investigation, which was part of the Commission's submission to the district court pursuant to Section 1103, was signed on October 17, 2002.

II

Members of the staff have reported information to the Commission which tends to show that from at least 1999 to the present:

A. Gemstar and its former and present officers, directors, employees, affiliates, and other persons or entities, directly or indirectly, in the offer or sale of, or in connection with the purchase or sale of Gemstar securities, may have employed a device, scheme, or artifice to defraud, made or obtained money or property by means of an untrue statement of material fact or omitted to state a material fact necessary in order to make the statements made, in light of the circumstances under which they were made, not misleading, or engaged in transactions, acts, practices or courses of business which operated or would operate as a fraud or deceit upon any person. As part of the aforesaid activities, such persons or entities may have, directly or indirectly, among other things, made materially false and misleading statements and may have traded in Gemstar stock while in possession of material nonpublic information in breach of a fiduciary or other duty arising out of a relationship of trust and confidence concerning, among other things, Gemstar's revenues and earnings or losses as set forth in Gemstar's 1999, 2000, 2001 and 2002 Forms 10-K and 10-Q;

B. Gemstar and its former and present officers, directors, employees, affiliates, and other persons or entities failed or caused the failure to file or filed or caused to be filed with the Commission annual reports on Form 10-K and quarterly reports on Form 10-Q which may have contained an untrue statement of material fact or may have omitted to state a material fact necessary, or may have failed to add such further material information as may be necessary in order to make the statements made, in light of the circumstances under which they were made, not misleading concerning, among other things, Gemstar's revenue and earnings or losses.

C. Gemstar and its former and present officers, directors, employees, affiliates, and other persons or entities may have failed to or caused the failure to:

1. make and keep books, records and accounts which, in reasonable detail, accurately and fairly reflected Gemstar's transactions and disposition of assets;

2. devise and maintain a system of internal accounting controls sufficient to provide reasonable assurances that transactions were recorded as necessary to permit preparation of financial statements in conformity with Generally Accepted Accounting Principles or any other criteria applicable to such statements, and to maintain accountability for assets;

D. Gemstar and its former and present officers, directors, employees, affiliates, and other persons or entities may have, directly or indirectly, falsified or caused to be falsified, books, records, or accounts required to be maintained by Gemstar.

E. Gemstar and its former and present officers, directors, employees, affiliates, and other persons or entities may have knowingly circumvented or knowingly failed to implement a system of internal accounting controls or knowingly falsified any book, record or account required to be maintained by Gemstar.

F. While engaged in the above described activities, such person or entities, directly or indirectly, made use of the mails or the means, instruments, or instrumentalities of transportation or communication in interstate commerce.

III

The Commission, having considered the staff's report and deeming such acts and practices, if true, to be in possible violation of Section 17(a) of the Securities Act of 1933 ("Securities Act") and Sections 10(b), 13(a), 13(b)(2)(A), 13(b)(2)(B) and 13(b)(5) of the Exchange Act and Rules 10b-5, 12b-20, 13a-1, 13a-13, and 13b2-1 thereunder, finds it necessary and appropriate and hereby:

ORDERS, pursuant to Section 20(a) of the Securities Act and Section 21(a) of the Exchange Act, that a private investigation be made to determine whether any persons or entities have engaged in, or are about to engage in, any of the reported acts or practices or any acts or practices of similar purport or object; .

The next step in this process is for the Commission to file with the district court an application for a temporary order pursuant to Section 1103. The Commission took this step on May 5, 2003, accompanied by a declaration in support executed by the Commission's attorney authorized to conduct the relevant investigation. Here are excerpts from the declaration, excerpts that sound very much like the allegations of probable cause to be found in a standard search warrant.

Since the Commission issued its Formal Order on October 17, 2002, the Commission's staff has taken investigative testimony from 57 witnesses (Author's note: I was one of them), for 105 days of testimony. The testimony has been taken throughout the United States.

The Commission's staff has scheduled the investigative testimony of additional witnesses.

Since the Commission issued its Formal Order on October 17, 2002, the Commission's staff has issued regulatory requests to brokerage firms for brokerage account information.

Since the Commission issued its Formal Order on October 17, 2002, the Commission's staff has issued over one hundred subpoenas for the production of documents. Pursuant to the subpoenas for the production of documents, the staff has received substantial document productions in response to the subpoenas.

On January 7, 1998, Henry Yuen entered into an Amended and Restated Employment Agreement ("Yuen's Employment Agreement") with Gemstar International Group, Ltd. and Gemstar Development Corp. (collectively with Gemstar-TV Guide International, Inc., "Gemstar"), a copy of which was attached.

Under Yuen's Employment Agreement, Yuen's initial base salary was $1 million, subject to annual increases that were based on Gemstar's reported financial results.

Yuen's Employment Agreement contained a formula under which Yuen's base salary could increase each year, depending upon annual percentage increases in Gemstar's consolidated revenues and consolidated net earnings, as reported in Gemstar's financial statements.

Yuen's Employment Agreement contained a provision for an annual merit bonus that was calculated using Gemstar's reported financial results. The formula used his adjusted base salary and the annual percentage increase, if any, in Gemstar's consolidated earnings before interest, taxes, depreciation and amortization ("EBITDA"). Yuen could elect to receive his merit bonus in the form of cash or stock options.

Yuen's Employment Agreement also included a provision for an annual incentive bonus that was calculated using Gemstar's reported financial results. The formula used his adjusted base salary and increases in Gemstar's consolidated earnings per share as reported in Gemstar's Forms 10-Q and 10-K. Yuen could elect to receive his annual incentive bonus in the form of cash or stock options.

Yuen's Employment Agreement provided Yuen with annual stock options.

During the investigation, the staff took Yuen's testimony on April 1, 2003, when he answered general background questions. The staff did not inquire into specific transactions in any detail. Yuen appeared again to provide testimony on April 23, 2003, at which time Yuen asserted his Fifth Amendment privilege against self-incrimination in response to all questions.

I have examined Forms W-2 issued to Yuen by Gemstar from 1999 through 2002 and have added the amounts of compensation reported on the Forms W-2 for those four years, which totals $37,849,002.35. The staff understands that this includes salary and wages, as well as monies related to the exercise of stock options.

The staff has analyzed brokerage records from Yuen's brokerage firm, including a “Master Agreement” dated March 27, 2002, and confirmations of transactions executed under that agreement. The brokerage records show that between April 3, 2002 and April 8, 2002, Yuen entered into “prepaid forward” transactions to dispose of 7 million shares of Gemstar stock. The brokerage records show that Yuen received an initial payment from the disposition of these 7 million shares of approximately $59 million.

On March 31, 1998, Elsie Leung entered into an Amended and Restated Employment Agreement with Gemstar International

Group, Ltd. and Gemstar Development Corp. ("Leung's Employment Agreement").

Under Leung's Employment Agreement, her initial base salary was $700,000, subject to annual increases based on Gemstar's financial results.

Leung's Employment Agreement included a formula to calculate annual increases in her base salary, which used annual percentage increases in Gemstar's consolidated revenues and consolidated net earnings as shown in Gemstar's financial statements.

Leung's Employment Agreement included a provision for an annual incentive bonus based upon Gemstar's financial results. The formula for calculating Leung's incentive bonus used her adjusted base salary and increases in Gemstar's consolidated earnings per share as reported in Gemstar's Forms 10-Q and 10-K.

Leung's Employment Agreement further provided Leung with annual stock options.

I have examined Forms W-2 issued to Leung by Gemstar from 1999 through 2002 and have added the amounts of compensation reported on the Forms W-2 for those four years, which totals $11,180,561.28.

On May 2, 2003, the staff provided notice to counsel for Gemstar, pursuant to Local Rule 7-19.1, that the Commission had authorized the staff to file an Application under Section 1103 of Sarbanes-Oxley Act of 2002 to seek a temporary order requiring Gemstar to escrow any extraordinary payments to its employees. The staff informed counsel for Gemstar that the Commission intended to file the Application on May 5, 2003, as early in the morning as possible.

In a supplemental memorandum in support of its application for a temporary order, the Commission made its compelling case that the payments at issue were not regular payments in the everyday operation or normal management of Gemstar. In many instances, the Commission simply pointed out what Yuen and Leung would have been normally entitled to, and then highlighted the differences arising from the suspect Termination Agreements that were not usual and ordinary, and thus "extraordinary." I highlight and quote from the memorandum:

I. INTRODUCTION

The Securities and Exchange Commission ("Commission") seeks a temporary order preventing Gemstar-TV Guide International, Inc., (Gemstar") [sic] from making any extraordinary payments to certain persons for a period of 45 days, under Section 1103 of the Sarbanes-Oxley Act of 2002. Respondent Gemstar does not oppose entry of an order maintaining the status quo. Intervenors Henry C. Yuen and Elsie Leung (collectively "Intervenors") oppose such an order because they contend:

(1) they should be heard before any order is entered;

(2) there is no reason to enter the order on an expedited basis; (3) the payments are not extraordinary under Section 1103; and (4) Section 1103 is unconstitutional.

II. ARGUMENT

A. The Restructuring Payments are Extraordinary Payments under Section 1103

The principal issue is whether the Restructuring Payments of $37.64 million in cash are extraordinary payments under Section 1103. Yuen and Leung admit that the payments are being made pursuant to their November 7, 2002 "Termination Agreements" with Gemstar that were the subject of at least five months of extended negotiation and approval by Gemstar's entire Board of Directors. Yuen and Leung also admit that the Restructuring Payments were made to affect their removal as Chief Executive Officer and Chief Financial Officer, respectively, and to remove control of Gemstar's Board of Directors from Yuen. The Restructuring Payments and their circumstances are so extraordinary that Yuen asserted his Fifth Amendment privilege to all questions about his compensation during testimony on April 25, 2003. Under these circumstances, the Restructuring Payments are extraordinary payments.

Yuen and Leung ignore the significant events that are the basis for the Restructuring Payments and focus only on the components which they characterize as ordinary payments made under "long standing contractual commitments." However, the operative agreements under which the Restructuring Payments are being made are the November 7, 2002 Termination Agreements, entered on the same day that the payments originally were to be disbursed by Gemstar. The Restructuring Payments are being made pursuant to the Termination Agreements, which by their terms supersede all other agreements between the parties. The restructuring was so significant that Gemstar issued a press release announcing it on October 8, 2002 and filed a Form 8-K on November 7, 2002.

Yuen and Leung also ignore that, in terms of relationship to annual compensation, the Restructuring Payments are extraordinary. Yuen is to receive a total of $56.7 million in cash and stock, of which $29.48 million is cash. This is more than five times Yuen's 2001 base salary of approximately $5 million a year. Leung is to receive $14.4 million in cash and stock, of which $8.16 million is cash. Similarly, this is more than six times Leung's 2001 base salary of $1.3 million.

There can be little dispute that the Restructuring Payments are not being made in a normal and usual course of business, but rather are "for an exceptional purpose or a special occasion."

Black's Law Dictionary, at p. 406 (Abridged Sixth Edition 1991). Indeed, if there were nothing remarkable about these payments, then Yuen could have testified freely about them on April 25, 2003; instead, he invoked his Fifth Amendment privilege against self-incrimination with respect to all questions about his compensation.

B. The Component Amounts Are Extraordinary Payments Under Section 1103

Yuen and Leung misdirect the Court away from the events and circumstances of the Restructuring Payments and the total $37.64 million in cash and focus instead on alleged components of the Restructuring Payments, which they identify as: (1) termination fees or severance payments; (2) accrued unpaid bonuses for 2001; (3) accrued unpaid salary; and (4) accrued unused vacation pay.

However, the Termination Agreements do not describe the Restructuring Payments as having the same components Yuen and Leung now advance to the Court: Yuen's Termination Agreement describes the payments as: "(i) a termination fee of $22,452,640 and (ii) $7,030,778 (in full and complete settlement for all unpaid salary, bonuses and unused vacation days due under the Current Employment Agreement or otherwise)." Leung's is similar. The Termination Agreements state that the single lump sum payments are a "settlement" of amounts due or "otherwise," and not merely simple contractual payments due in the ordinary course. The description in the Termination Agreements is consistent with Intervenors' admission that the Restructuring Payments were the subject of "extended" negotiations, and that component amounts that make up the lump sum settlement payments in the Termination Agreements are largely different than amounts due under their employment agreements.

Yuen's and Leung's argument that the Court should look at each component in isolation, and not in context of the events and the governing documents, should be rejected. Under their argument, an extraordinary payment would escape Section 1103 if made up of components that can be characterized as usual or ordinary. Thus, if the Court finds that the "vacation pay" component is not extraordinary, then in the future an issuer and its employees will simply call suspect extraordinary payments "vacation pay" to evade the statute. Section 1103 should not be read in a restrictive manner that would render it meaningless, but rather it should be read broadly to affect the remedial purposes of the federal securities laws. See, e.g., SEC v. Zandford, 535 U.S. 813, 122 S.Ct. 1899, 153 L.Ed.2d 1 (2002).

1. The termination fees are extraordinary payments

Yuen and Leung admit that the bulk of the funds are a termination fee or severance payment, but do not provide any specific arguments why these are not extraordinary payments under Section 1103. Yuen and Leung admit that the amount of termination fees was negotiated and are substantially different than the severance payments they may have been entitled to under their existing employment agreements. The Termination Agreements provide that Yuen is to receive a "termination fee" of $22.45 million, and Leung a "termination fee" of $6,957,953.

The "termination fees" are the amounts agreed to, after extended negotiation between Gemstar, Yuen, and Leung, as the amounts Gemstar must pay to terminate Yuen and Leung. Generally, the termination of a chief executive officer or chief financial officer is an extraordinary event, usually accompanied by a public announcement and a Form 8-K filing, as it was here.

2. The accrued unpaid bonuses for 2001

Bonuses are clearly the type of extraordinary payments encompassed by Section 1103. A bonus is not an ordinary and usual payment, but rather a "consideration or premium paid in addition to what is strictly due" and a "premium or extra or irregular remuneration." As Senator Lott commented about Section 1103: "While an investigation is underway, basically rewards were given to these corporate executives." Any common-sense interpretation of a bonus understands that it is a special reward for meeting or surpassing goals.

Yuen and Leung's 2001 bonuses are exactly the type of payments that should be frozen: their bonuses are rewards for Gemstar's 2001 reported financial results. The Commission is investigating whether Gemstar's 2001 financial results were fraudulently overstated. Since Yuen and Leung (and others) signed and filed Gemstar's 2001 Form 10-K on April 1, 2002, Gemstar has restated and reversed substantial revenue items contained in the 2001 Form 10-K. The very set of events Section 1103 was designed to prevent is implicated by the bonus payments: while the Commission is attempting to determine whether Gemstar's 2001 financial results were overstated and fraudulent, Yuen and Leung are demanding to be paid for those results.

Under their employment agreements, the calculation of Yuen and Leung's bonuses is tied directly to Gemstar's reported financial results. Yuen's "merit bonus" is calculated using his adjusted base salary and Gemstar's percentage increase in EBITDA (earnings before interest, taxes, depreciation, and amortization). Yuen and Leung each had an identical provision in their employment agreements for an "incentive bonus," calculated based on Gemstar's reported financial results.

3. The accrued unpaid salary

The unpaid salary component of the settlement amount is, like the bonus payment component, directly dependent upon Gemstar's reported 2001 financial statements that are under investigation by the Commission. Yuen and Leung's employment agreements included a formula for the annual adjustment of their base salary. Under that formula, if consolidated revenues or consolidated net earnings increase, then Yuen and Leung's base salary is increased by a proportional amount.

The calculation of the "catch-up" salary based upon allegedly fraudulent financial statements is, again, exactly the type of "reward" about which Section 1103 is concerned. Gemstar has restated hundreds of millions of dollars of revenues from multiple transactions since Yuen and Leung entered into the Termination Agreements. To the extent Gemstar's reported financial results have been overstated for many years (as indicated by the restatements), Yuen and Leung's compensation and bonuses are terminally infected with those overstatements.

4. The accrued unused vacation pays

The extraordinary nature of the vacation pay amount in the settlement is revealed by the context. In the ordinary course, an employee would take their vacation time during a year and receive their salary while on vacation. The employee is paid accrued but unused vacation pay only on a special occasion-when their employment is terminated. [Sic] But for the restructuring and their removal, Yuen and Leung had no contractual rights, under their employment agreements, to be paid for accrued but unused vacation.

V

Given the context of Section 1103 and the narrowly defined, regulated, and targeted area to which it applies, I conclude that Congress' use of the term "extraordinary" in connection to payments being made by the issuer to those insiders possibly under investigation for potential securities fraud does not constitute a legal or a constitutional infirmity in this statute. "Extraordinary" simply means, in plain language, out of the ordinary. In this context-and the context is the key- “out of the ordinary” simply means a payment made not in the customary or normal pursuit of the regular trade or business of the issuer under scrutiny, but in response to an irregular or abnormal demand of the moment that reasonably appears to have been provoked or motivated by or connected to the possible violations of securities laws that triggered the investigation.

There is no need necessarily to engage in metaphysical inquiries about what is ordinary in another company or to look to some sort of an industry standard to ascertain the meaning of this provision. One can simply look at the business of the issuer and determine whether the payments under scrutiny directly advance the issuer's normal business objectives, or whether the payment reasonably appears to be damage control, hush money, taking financial advantage of the fraud, cover-up, looting, etc.

The district court had it exactly right. The court looked in context at (1) the circumstances of the payment, (2) the purpose of the payment, and (3) the size of the payment. The court concluded in a thorough, thoughtful, and well-reasoned, 23-page decision that the Commission “has met its burden” “under almost any standard.”

The court correctly focused on the nature, purpose, and circumstances of the payments and determined that they had nothing to do with Gemstar's ordinary business. The court accurately noted that:

[t]he payments were negotiated over a five-month period and involved the participation of the Gemstar Board, a Special Committee, and outside consultants. The Board, the Special Committee, and the Intervenors Yuen and Leung were each represented by separate sets of counsel. Additionally, the termination agreements were executed as part of the process of removing Leung and Yuen from their positions as Gemstar Officers.

The court concluded that the termination agreements and the disputed payments "are anything but ordinary." I agree. Why? Because the measure of "extraordinary" is what ordinarily goes on in the process of the issuer's business, and these facts are clearly unusual and extraordinary. As the Commission's supplemental memorandum points out, the negotiated Termination Agreement payments here are five and six times greater than Yuen's and Leung's base salary, the component amounts that make up the lump sum payments are different than the amounts due under their employment agreements, the termination fees are different from what they may have been entitled to under existing agreements, the bonuses are fruit of the alleged fraudulent financial results, and the vacation pay item did not exist under their contracts. One would not expect benefits like these to be flowing from corporate assets to executives resigning under fire. This scenario is not business as usual. It appears to be looting. I believe, as did the district court, that Gemstar's execution of its overall business objectives and ordinary management of its business operations did not entail terminating its CEO and CFO in the shadow of misstated revenues, misleading public statements, securities fraud investigations, plunging stock prices, and public relations debacles, not to mention Yuen's and Leung's inability to certify Gemstar's books as accurate. If these mega-suspicious payments were not "extraordinary," the word needs either to be redefined or to be taken out of our dictionaries. Gemstar's Form 8-K filings raise red flags all over the place.

Do we really expect the government to offer evidence of what constitutes "usual or ordinary payments to a CEO and a CFO under same or similar circumstances," i.e., under threat of delisting, in a fight with its independent auditor, and under investigation for having misstated revenues, cooked the books, defrauded investors, employees and the market, and possibly committed a basket full of crimes? Why would this be necessary? On reflection, the idea that a court needs somehow to have evidence of a "norm for corporate decision-making of this type," i.e., rampaging fraud and a world of trouble, seems off the mark. In some cases, one might need to look to a norm, but not this one. Legal "probable cause" statements do not need information about how normal people act to create a reasonable suspicion with respect to the targeted suspects. These insiders appear, from the record submitted to the district court, to be pirates engaged in cookie jar mismanagement of Gemstar. The Commission subsequently sued them for multiple securities fraud violations, seeking anti-fraud injunctions, civil money penalties, and disgorgement of ill-gotten gains, including salaries, bonuses, and proceeds from the sale of stock-each one of which is at the epicenter of the payments at issue. The Commission's complaint alleges that because their compensation was linked to Gemstar's reported financial results, Yuen and Leung reaped millions of dollars in financial gains-in excess salary, bonuses, and options-from their fraudulent manipulations of Gemstar's revenues, to the tune of an overstatement of those revenues by at least $223 million.

Congress designed Section 1103 to add teeth to the Commission's ability to perform its mission. It ensures that recovery by way of disgorgement, etc., is effective rather than empty. As for the importance of disgorgement, we have said,

Disgorgement plays a central role in the enforcement of the securities laws. The effective enforcement of the federal securities laws requires that the Commission be able to make violations unprofitable. The deterrent effect of a Commission enforcement action would be greatly undermined if securities law violators were not required to disgorge illicit profits. By deterring violations of the securities laws, disgorgement actions further the Commission's public policy mission of protecting investors and safeguarding the integrity of the markets. Although the Commission at times may use the disgorged proceeds to compensate injured victims, this does not detract from the public nature of Commission enforcement actions: the touchstone remains the fact that public policies are served, and the public interest is advanced by the litigation.

Finally, the proof of the extraordinary nature of this pudding is in the eating. The multimillion-dollar, suspicious-resignation Termination Agreements, which Yuen and Leung claim are not extraordinary, were approved and signed by Jonathan Orlick, Gemstar's General Counsel, now also a defendant in a civil fraud complaint filed by the SEC, involving fraud allegedly arising out of this same tarnished episode in Gemstar's existence. So much for the ordinary course of business argument.

Appendix C
Acquisition of Funding

Traditionally new ventures are funded through a series of predictable steps including all or most of the following:

1. Personal financing often through the heavy use of credit cards
2. Friends and family (where all investors either know the entrepreneur or are related to him/her.)
3. Extended friends and family (this kind of funding is often overlooked and can be very dangerous, as described in two of the cases below.)
4. Early professional or angel investing
5. Additional funding often treated as a "Series A"

In every one of these steps the underlying assertion is that the funding round will create enough additional value to produce a significant return for the investors in that round. Another way of saying that the "pre-round valuation" will increase each time.

Notes on the Author

Dave Carlson recently retired from the position of Senior Vice President and Chief Technology Officer of IHS (now IHS-Markit). During his five years at IHS, the company grew from about $550 million to $1.3 billion; a compounded annual sales and profit growth rate of about 20%. His responsibilities included all product development, internal business applications, content management systems, world-wide infrastructure and technology architecture and strategies including mobile devices and cloud computing. IHS made 38 acquisitions during this time with an acquisition cost of about $1.5 billion. All technology-related due diligence and reporting was done by his team and him. As a member of the CEO's Executive Leadership Team he attended all meetings related to all of the acquisitions and personally led all technology-related discussions.

He has served in senior technology positions in several other companies including Ingram Micro which grew from about $8 billion in annual sales to about $28 billion in the three years he was there. He led Kmart's technology revolution between 1985 and 1995 and installed more than 20,000 remote computer systems and 50,000 lanes of UPC scanning during that time. While he was at Kmart the company was profitable. As a senior retail executive at Kmart, he was instrumental in moving the industry toward technical standards for product barcoding, electronic data interchange and logistical standards.

Over his career he has managed technology investments, licenses and total spending of more than $4 billion and more than 4,000 professional employees involved with software and infrastructure development and support. He also has managed sales forces for both direct and indirect channels. He participated in the due diligence analysis of more than 50 companies with revenues ranging from $2 million to $500 million. He has also served as an executive and board member of several start-up companies. He co-founded and had his first successful exit from Information Control Systems, Inc. (Ann Arbor) in 1969.

He recently retired as Chairman of the Orange County Audit Oversight Committee (OCAOC) and was its longest serving member; having served more than 20 years. On September 26, 2017 the State of California presented him with a Senate Resolution honoring his services. He was also a member of the Board of Directors, Electronic Resources Limited, a public Singapore company, a member of the Board of Trustees of Adrian College, Adrian, Michigan and a Guest Lecturer at the London School of Economics. In 1990 and 1991 he made presentations in Moscow on proposed technical standards. His visits were sponsored by the Central Committee on Publishing of the Soviet Union during General Secretary Mikhail Gorbachev's "Glasnost" and "Perestroika" initiatives. In April of 2012 he was a guest of the Chinese government as a member of a delegation of US business people that attended conferences in several Chinese cities. In Suzhou, China he gave a speech on Customer-focused Cloud Computing with a short introduction in Mandarin. Other travel includes more than 75 trips to Europe and several trips to the Middle East and Asia.

Dr. Carlson holds a BS in Mathematics (1964), an M.S. in Industrial Administration (1966) and a Ph.D. in Engineering (1975); all from the University of Michigan where he also did post-doctoral work in Financial Policy and taught Experimental Psychology and Computer Systems Analysis & Design. He recently took additional academic work in dispute resolution at the Pepperdine Law School and attended the Directors College at the Stanford

University Law School Rock Center for Corporate Governance.

He has always been interested in business ethics and first taught a class on the subject at Graceland College in Lamoni, Iowa in 1966.

His industry awards include the Carnegie-Mellon/American Management Systems' "Award for Achievements in Managing Information Technology;" the Society for Information Management "Partners in Leadership" Award and the Smithsonian Institution "In Search of New Heroes" Award. His contributions to developing and implementing technology standards include serving on the Board of Governors of the Uniform Code Council (Now GS1, administrators of the UPC and its symbol) and Chairing the Voluntary Inter-Industry Communications Standards Committee (now also part of GS1).

He holds U.S. Patent #5,892,434. In 1994, he co-authored "Information Technology in the Service Society: A Twenty-First Century Lever," as a member of the National Academies of Sciences' Committee to Study the Impact of Information Technology on the Performance of Service Activities.

He served in the U.S. Army twice and is a veteran of the Vietnam era.

He is a very active member of the Orange Coast Unitarian Universalist Church in Costa Mesa California.

Questions for Discussion

1. Many of the chapters describe issues of corporate governance. What are the obligations of a board member even when the control of the company rests with the founder/entrepreneur and the board member knows that he or she can be replaced at any time?

2. In a privately held company, like many of those described in this book, do board members have a responsibility to look below the surface of financial statements to ensure the practices are ethical and legal?

3. In a privately held company, like many of those described in this book, do employees and executives have a responsibility to look below the surface of financial statements and operations to ensure the practices are ethical and legal?

4. In Chapter 12, a situation is described that involves a co-founder bringing in a large temporary staff for one day to help convince a venture capital firm to invest. If you saw this happening what, if any, actions would you take?

5. If you are invited to a meeting with either customers or shareholders at which the entrepreneur grossly exaggerates his credentials, his accomplishments or the status and future of the company, what are your obligations, if any?

6. If, as a minority shareholder, you come across information that may reflect illegal activities on the part of the company, would you have an obligation to share it with other shareholders or the board?

7. Startup companies often raise many rounds of funding. As an employee during one of these rounds do you have an obligation to make your concerns about material overstatements known to potential investors?

8. Did the author violate business ethics when he took the findings of activities in Chapter 1 directly to the IRS after the board rejected his recommendations?

9. If you as an employee realize that the founder is grossly overstating his or her ability to provide value for a customer what are your options and ultimately your obligations?

10. If you are a major contributor to a business plan which is then circulated and subsequently there are changes in the assumptions which materially affect the plan, what are your obligations?

11. If you'd been asked to be a member of the board of a start-up which had been created by a very good friend and you see that friend displaying characteristics described in this book as hubris, what are your obligations to him or

her? And, if you decide to take action, what approach is likely to get the best result?

12. Chapter 3 describes a situation where the founder presents the CEO with a request for a substantial amount of money which was not included in the use of funds statement. Even though the corporate attorney allowed the transaction to proceed was the CEO obligated to revisit all of the significant investors pointing out this material change in the use of funds?

13. Are questions about felony convictions, when interviewing entrepreneurs or investors, too intrusive and not particularly relevant to possible transactions?

14. Jerre Stead and Howard Matthews are both mentioned in the book as extraordinary CEOs. Based on your experience with managers and executives at all levels, what are the most important behaviors executives need to exhibit to accomplish the objectives of the organization?

Index